MW01531647

To: Bro. Sidney -
a great friend in
Christ -
Calvin L. Porter
4/14/11

Beaten But Not Broken

YAHWEH Jireh- "The Lord Provides"

C. G. Coker

authorHOUSE®

AuthorHouse™
1663 Liberty Drive, Suite 200
Bloomington, IN 47403
www.authorhouse.com
Phone: 1-800-839-8640

© 2007 C. G. Coker. All rights reserved.

No part of this book may be reproduced, stored in a retrieval system, or transmitted by any means without the written permission of the author.

First published by AuthorHouse 7/18/2007

ISBN: 978-1-4343-2564-8 (sc)

Library of Congress Control Number: 2007905041

Printed in the United States of America
Bloomington, Indiana

This book is printed on acid-free paper.

In Memory of My Parents,
Patsy Lee Mosley Coker
And Lee Earnest Coker

Because of them, I am what I am. Because of them, I am committed to a relationship with God. I love family and refuse to be a slave to materialism. There is no shame in being born into poverty or being black and living in a society dominated by white supremacists. No man, woman, boy, or girl should ever be ashamed of their color or nationality. Understand that many have endured similar circumstances. It is not just a racial issue; it should also be categorized as a byproduct of a class society. There is no need to ponder "what if." I had my parents, each for a specific time, and then they were gone, but the wisdom and understanding passed down from God to them will live in me forever. Yes, it was sufficient for my brothers, sisters, and me. The memories of our past at times still are quite painful, some of which I cannot share in this book, but they have produced a more acceptable present and left us with a great hope and faith in the future.

Pop, the baby boy

To My Sisters and Brothers

To each of my brothers and sisters, dead or alive: there is a special candle that burns in my heart for each of you. I write these pages to signify some of the struggles, but more importantly, our victories. So as you read this, you will think of similar events or the events that I fail to mention. I want it stated for the record that I am proud to be your brother and that I really appreciate each of you for the times in which you looked out for me and prayed for me. And I know you are praying for me, loving me. I want you to know that I love you and pray that our love for each other carries through to our children and our children's children.

Calvin

To My Children: Nathan, Ashley, and Derrick

Well, guys, when you read this book you will see your dad going through some of the stages of life—some things bad, some things good, and maybe many unbelievable things based on what you are accustomed to today. I wanted you to have an account of my life. I want you to know that the hate of racism is real but sometimes black also. You have the power to overcome it and any other obstacle that comes in front of you. I want you to notice and truly adopt a principle that was passed to me by my mother, and that is to acknowledge God and hold Him dear in your hearts. As you read this book, laugh and cry too, because that was life and is life. Each of you has been blessed to be where you are today. When you fall down, look in these pages and know that you can get back up. I love you,

Dad

To My Wife, Cynthia

Thank you so much for helping me to be able to express myself and helping me to see that it is okay for black men to cry, not just on sad occasions but on happy ones too. Throughout the years of writing this book, I have grown as each page liberated me by setting me free from pieces of yesterday. Thank you for sticking with me through all of the ungodly times as well as the godly times. Thank you for persistently urging me for years to write this book and tell my story. Your excitement, which sometimes seems to have exceeded mine, pushed me to keep the dream alive and provide this book as a resource to our kids, brothers and sisters, and others to know how important it is to have a strong family. So as you now have this book, you have a piece of me and probably now you can see why our kids do some of the things that they do. You are my wife, my lover, my friend; may you enjoy this book as my love for you grows.

Loving you,
Calvin

Table of Contents

Chapter 1 Pop, the Baby Boy

I was told that I was born at the edge of a cotton field. You see, black mothers of the South during that day worked in the cotton fields even when pregnant, and my mother was no exception. She worked as much as she was able, even though she really wasn't able. Many days she must have told herself that she was able in order to help the family out just a little bit more. Therefore, on this day, September 8, 1959, about ten miles in a southwest direction outside Selma, Alabama, I was born to my mother at the end of a cotton row. My mother was forty-one at the time of my birth, and I was number fourteen, the last of the children of Patsy Lee Mosley Coker and Lee Earnest Coker, and I was given the title of Pop, the baby boy.

Who could like such a title? My youngest sister was glad to pass the title on to me, as everyone would call me "the baby of the family." Even now, when I go to the South, older people there still refer to me as the "baby of the family." These same people can't remember your name, the day of the week, or even their own name at times, but they remember that I am the baby of the family of Patsy and Lee Earnest. Even my own sisters and brothers would then and still now refer to me as the baby boy; Even today, they have trouble seeing me as an equal adult able and ready to offer them advice as well as they do to me.

The baby of the family is the least respected, almost always ignored by older sisters and brothers when it comes to opinion, and now that I was on the scene, my youngest sister, who was still older than me, could have someone to pass orders down to or try to be the boss of. There is a good side to this also. Being the baby of the family meant things were not as bad for me as they had been for my brothers and sisters; there was some preferential treatment for the baby of the family. Don't get me wrong; it was bad for me. But it was much worse for my older brothers and sisters.

They saw much more hardship than I did and worked in the fields (including the cotton fields) more than I would. They faced much more racial bigotry than I did and were subjected to much more abuse than I was. For us, it was stamped in our upbringing to leave the South after high school and go to a place where we would have a chance to be equals and live the American dream of freedom, peace, liberty, and prosperity.

For many blacks who stayed in Selma, life might have appeared hopeless because it seemed as if change would be impossible. The white establishment in charge was running things with an iron fist, and the Southern law permitted it with unfair laws such as Jim Crow. So many of these people called themselves Christians, but how could they serve the same God that we served? How could they violate the first law of God, love others with such disregard and still maintain their secret and corporate devotion to the Almighty? Sorry. I get sidetracked sometimes, even today because these people still exist, still claiming to have a personal tower with God, but the evidence is unseen.

They also tell me that I was born with a veil over my face. Doctors today would call it the mucus discharge when a baby is born; the women who were there to help my mother bring me into this world called it a veil because it was dark and covered my face. There was a saying that any baby born with such a veil over its face would be able to see things that others couldn't see. Growing up, I never gave this a thought, but over the years, I do believe that God has shown me many things to help me focus and move in the right direction (sometimes pleasant and sometimes not so pleasant). I believe that my mother took it as a sign from God because the majority of the memories that I have of my mother deal with her teaching me the Bible and about God and developing my gifts to serve Him.

As far back as I can remember; there are images of my mother teaching me from the Bible. My attention span was very short, but she was relentless, never giving up and quite often telling and reading to me the same story; over and over again. This was also reinforced by listening to gospel music and preachers on the radio, which seemed to always be playing during the mornings. My mother also taught me that the Lord would take care of me. She would say, "I know you don't really understand it now, but as long as I am alive, I will keep telling you that the Lord will take care of you." She would also say, "Someday it'll make sense to you."

My mother was a strong black woman cursed with many health issues, but they were all secondary when it came to her commitment to the family. I mentioned how she worked the fields while pregnant with me. I was number fourteen, and she didn't start doing this with me but with my brothers and sisters. Through the hardship and agony of it all, I never remember her complaining about how poor we were or how we had to do without. She was sick very often. The doctors said that she had pelvic cancer, but they really had no plan of healing her, and as a result, many experimental surgeries were done on my mother. You may have heard recently that black women receive the worst medical care from the medical profession, but try to think back and look at this racial-prejudiced white society of Selma, Alabama; the fact that she was black automatically meant that she would not receive the best care or be able to go to the finer hospitals or have access to the best doctors. Her body must have been worn and torn as well from having fourteen children the hard way in the South; there was no such thing as well-baby care or visiting the doctor, no sedative or epidural. The hard scars of having so many babies would complicate any sickness present. This was during the early '60s in rural Selma, Alabama, but for us black people; it might as well have been the 1800s.

However, my mother was a strong black woman through the trials and tribulations of cancer, of being overworked and underappreciated by my father, of never having any time for herself but always for someone else; yes, my mother was a strong black woman. I remember how she would give to neighbors and many times people she didn't know. During that day, prisoners would be working by cleaning and building the highway. In the South during the '60s, prisoners wore stripes and did hard work. They fixed and worked on the highways and kept them clean. The prisoners were always black or

Indian. (This was because no white prisoners were not put with the other races. I think I can make a safe assumption and say that as long as there were prisoners of races other than white, the white prisoners never really did the hard work, unless they did something to really tick off the warden or guards.) She would give water and food to them (even though we did not have much for ourselves); many of them would thank her, and some would remember her when they got out of prison. My mother was very generous and caring to others; I would like to think that we kids have those traits as well, and to a large degree, we do, but I also know that within us there also exists the wrath of Lee Earnest Coker, my father (more about him later).

When others were in school or on days that she just couldn't make it to the fields, my mother was with me. She always read the Bible to me; her Bible had many pictures, and we had a relationship such that Bible time was expected. It was through this experience that I learned to read by matching many of the pictures with the stories and through the repetition of hearing my mother read the passages to me. Many times, she would read and ask me questions, and the majority of the time I could not answer the questions, but I remember her saying that one day I would answer all of these questions and more. But I was just two, three, and four, so that kind of talk made no sense to me either.

My dad always seemed to be close to stressing out. He was like an Arizona desert facing a long drought, just waiting for a spark. None of us kids wanted to set him off; it would just happen. I think that I must have really tested him one Christmas Eve when I was four years old. At the end of each year, my dad would always kill a hog so that we would have meat for the winter and spring. We had no modern facility to butcher the hog. We had no running water, plumbing or gas to speed this process up; therefore, it was an all-day event that sometimes went well into the night. There would be big black pots of hot water boiling over on outside fires. Hot boiling water would then be poured over the hog. Yes, I forgot a step: killing the hog. Well, it wasn't pretty and appeared to take a long time. Later on, when I got older, my dad would shoot the hog in the head, but early on, he didn't because shooting the hog could damage some of the meat in the head. With the exception of the hair and body waste, every other part of the hog was used. I don't want you to think that my father enjoyed killing these animals, but he viewed it as a necessity to feed his family; he would pray before killing each animal and thank God for providing what we did have.

You would not believe how efficient we had become with this process. My father had built a smokehouse out of old leftover materials from his sharecrop work for the man. Within the smokehouse, we would hang hog shanks, hams, ribs, and loins from the top of the shed. We would keep a slow fire burning just enough to keep the small shed smoky. After a period of time set by my father, we would then take the meat down, rub it with salt, and put it in a big wooden chest located in the smokehouse. After a period of time, we would sometimes hang the meat back up and smoke it some more.

We even made use of the brain, which we would fry with eggs. If it was a male, we would fry the testicles (the proper name is mountain oysters) and have them for breakfast, but my father would never let my sisters eat the mountain oysters for various reasons, which I would rather not even try to explain. The intestine (also known as chitterlings) was also eaten normally around New Years Day. We would grind up the meat from the head and make "hog-head cheese." (It's an acquired taste.) Early on, most of the meat was keep outside in the smokehouse, since it was colder out there than in our icebox (not to be confused with a refrigerator, which runs on electricity; it runs on cold blocks of ice). This was what we had in 1964. We made our own pork rinds by cutting up the outer skin of the hog, which was about two inches thick. At the same time of preparing the outer skin, a big black pot would be put over an extremely hot fire. Water would be put in the black pot, and the older people would put the cut-up strips of hog fat into the black pot. We had to keep the fire extremely hot to cook the fat down to pork rinds; this took hours. When finished, we would separate the pork rinds from the pig oil. The oil would be used for cooking and the pork rinds would be put in a huge barrel for the family to eat.

Well after the hog had been slaughtered and prepared for the smokehouse, we kids had been tasked to burn all the brush. In the middle of this task, my brother Howard and I were playing, jumping across the flames. I had on a new pair of overalls. (You only got one new pair per year sometimes.) He jumped, then I jumped; then he jumped, then I jumped; and out of nowhere, my dad jumped, and the next thing I knew, my dad was rolling me around in the dirt. I heard something like screams of an unknown tongue coming out of my father's mouth. I then looked behind myself and noticed that the fire had burned a good portion of my new overalls, and at that time, I realized and understood what the yelling was all about. It was Christmas Eve, and I was about to get the gift that I would not wish on any child, whether naughty or nice.

I think the whole family was thinking of the crucifix rather than Christmas. It was like the anger that my father had about the whole day was directed toward me. I blocked out all that my father was yelling at me but could not block out the pain of the switch (a small branch from a nearby tree). My father destroyed the first one on me, got another one, and began to continue whipping me without mercy. I remember my mother pleading for my father to stop, but he was a black man in the South and told her to go inside and not try to tell him how to raise his children. I thank my mother for stepping in because even though he had said that, he soon quit. And then again, maybe he just got tired; after all, it had been a long day.

I was very worried because I was sure that I had been bad and Santa would not be coming to bring me anything. As I nursed my blisters, I cried myself to sleep, worried about my error made earlier in the day. When morning came, my dad was a different person; he was happy and joyous and had not forgotten about me for Christmas. I don't remember what I got that year, but I do remember that I loved my dad and mother even more because they had shown me not only the cause of my mistakes but also the mercy of their love. That's the way it was; we had swift and tough punishment when we did wrong, but it never would last for long periods of time.

Christmas was such a special time for us because that was the time when an older sibling would usually come home to visit. Santa could bring no gift that would match the joy of having older siblings come home. It was a special family time when we celebrated the birth of the Messiah. For us kids, we hoped to be visited by Santa Claus. It didn't matter what we got; it was just good to know that we were going to get something. It was never anything huge, but we knew that whatever it was, it required an effort from my father. He worked hard to give us a special Christmas, even thought he knew he would not get much from us kids; his joy was to see the excitement of his kids on Christmas Day.

One tradition was to give each child a Christmas bag. (We never had Christmas stockings.) During the week of Christmas, my father would buy a box of Washington State apples and a box of oranges, Brazil nuts, candy corn, and orange slices. A little money was put away for this a little bit at a time during the fall. Even today, I joyously remember the Christmas bag. Whenever I smell apples, I think of those Christmas sacks that we were given during my youth. We didn't get such treats often, so this was a very special event that all the children looked forward to with awaiting eyes. During this time, the fresh smell of apples and oranges was throughout the house, and even now when I smell apples and oranges, it reminds me of Christmas when I was a little boy.

We all knew that we had to safeguard our Christmas bag; leaving it unattended could have devastating side effects. To help protect our bags, we all talked about licking everything in the bag to discourage others from partaking of goodies from someone else's bag. This helped tremendously but not entirely. We all knew that there was no protection for oranges, and licking some of the candy would mean that it had to be eaten right away or it would have to be thrown away.

Two events always made me feel horrible. The lesser of the two was when I would do something that really upset my mother. Her punishments would always seem to be of biblical proportion and seemed to relate to some lesson for me. I loved to throw rocks at moving objects, and one day I hit a moving object, a baby chick. I killed a baby chick. When I saw that the chick was not moving, I knew something of a psychological nature was going to occur. I got a behind lashing, but that was just the start. When it came to punishment, my mother obeyed every implication of the Word by not sparing the rod and following up with memorable principles of discipline. She made me pick up the little chick. This wasn't as easy as you would think, because the mother hen was standing by, but my mother was insistent, "Pick him up, and bring him in the house!" When I got close to the dead chick, the mother hen would come after me; this must have been funny to my mother because she went inside and waited for me. Therefore, I took this as an opportunity to throw a few more rocks at the mother hen as I approached the chick that I had slain.

I picked up the chick with one hand and used the other to throw rocks at the mother hen. The only problem was that I needed another hand to open the kitchen screen door because the mother hen was after me. Therefore, I did what any four-year-old would do. I screamed and yelled my lungs out, hoping that my mother would come and rescue me. When she opened the door, I flew in, leaving the mother hen outside. I was then commanded to pour hot water over the dead chick and pick off all the feathers. My mother cleaned and gutted the chick. When dinnertime came, I had to eat the baby chick. My guilt was great, but I learned an important lesson, which is to never kill or harm an animal for fun. I found out that night that guilt didn't taste like chicken.

The *most* horrid event was when my mother would be so sick that she could not spend time with me on the Bible. She just lay in the bed, speechless, lifeless, and unaware of any activities around her. Often she would go into comas; this caused me great fear because I wondered if she would wake up. During these times, I would try to match the pictures in the Bible up with the stories that she had taught me earlier. My next feat would be to attempt cooking little simple things such as eggs, grits, toast, fatback, etc. One time I remember my mother going into a deep sleep; I mistook it for a coma, did my Bible study and then went to the kitchen to attempt cooking. While standing in a chair over a wooden stove, I put two eggs in a boiler with water on the stove. I thought that I saw a ghost moving toward me; no such luck. It was my mother with that biblical discipline. I don't remember what she actually did, but I know I made sure the next time that it was safe and clear to try to cook.

I remember talking to my mother about some ungodly behavior of my father. I went everywhere with my father. When he would be on one knee praying in church, I would be on my knees right beside him. When he went to visit the sick, I would go too. This is what caused me great stress one day because my father visited another woman, and I don't mean in a godly way. I could tell that there was something wrong. When we got home, I told my mother about it, and to my surprise, she said that it was all right, that my father needed companionship that she was unable to give. I remember this as if it was yesterday. I said "Sister [what we called our mother], that ain't right of Lenearst [what we called our father]; that's wrong." Once again, the strong black woman of the South said to me, "Respect your father, love your father, cause I got to leave here to be with the Lord, and I forgive him."

When I was approaching the age of five, I remember seeing my mother crying in bed, and I asked her why she was crying; she told me that she was going to be leaving soon. I replied to her that I knew she was going to die and asked her who was going to take care of me. She asked me how I knew, and I told her that it was just something that I knew. She then told me not to fret or worry, that she had talked it over with the Lord and that He would take care of me. My mother also said to me, "Never stop seeing what God shows you." I believed my mother and to this day have the same belief.

Not long afterward, my mother went into Good Samaritan Hospital in Selma, Alabama for the last time. The hospital had a policy that children were not allowed in rooms of people who were sick like my mother, so my older brother Eugene picked up Sanguretta my youngest sister) and me and put us in through the window. I didn't know everything that was going on, but I could feel the pain, anguish, and grief of my father, grandmother, sisters, and brothers. My mother hugged Sanguretta and me for the last time. The next time I remember seeing my mother was at her funeral. The coffin was open and I saw my mother for the very last time. Seeing my mother like that didn't scare me, but seeing my father beaten and broken down, crying, and yelling did; up to this time, I had never seen my father cry or show such pain and sorrow. It was unreal to see him that way; he had always been a rock. I thought he was not capable of showing such emotion or feeling.

You see, my dad had taught us as his father had taught him—that a black man in the South had to be strong, and this meant not showing any weakness, and crying was a weakness. As black males, we were taught not to show tears or fear. To go further, we were not taught to show emotions or affection.

I never remember my father hugging me or telling me that he loved me. I'm sure that he did love us, but there was just this great weight on his shoulders that was on the shoulders of every black man of the South during that period, to follow the protocol and be strong. Within the black culture of the South, it was a sign of weakness for a man to cry or show much emotion, except in church.

Even after my mother's funeral, my father never told us that he loved us. It just wasn't in him to say it. My grandmother on my mother's side, Amy Bell, was a source of comfort for us during this time and only lived about a mile away. Don't get me wrong; she wasn't your typical grandmother either, but when it came to us kids, she was more understanding than my father. I guess that she had compassion for us, something that I don't think my father could really tolerate; in his eyes, compassion was a sign of weakness.

Somehow, we got past that day, the next, and the day after, but I will never forget my mother, and perhaps that is why I remember those days so well. Today I have a collection of songs by Mahalia Jackson because she was one of my mother's favorite gospel singers. I also have the memory of my mother giving water to the prisoners that were cutting the grass on the side of the road and the times that my mother gave bread to the homeless traveler passing through.

My mother always loved flowers, especially roses; because of this, I have always planted the red traditional rose bush at each house of residence. These are the type of memories I have of my mother. A giver to all and a taker of none, Patsy Lee Mosley Coker was my mother and I am glad to have had her as my mother.

Chapter 2 My God, My God, Why Have You Forsaken Us?

It didn't take long to find out that being poor was not the biggest problem for blacks in the Selma area. There was a much bigger problem lurking over the entire South; it was like being covered with a heavy blanket in a bad dream. It was like a dream where you are in a room filled with smoke, choking, clinging for fresh air, and just wanting to break free, but this room has no windows or door to escape.

Unfortunately, it was not a dream, and the blanket was real. It was the covering of a racist South, which proudly endorsed and enforced white supremacy. As a little boy, I remember Klan rallies just like kids today would remember a Christmas parade. The good old white folks of Selma and surrounding communities made it clear that they didn't like black folks and that black folks had better remember their place. There would be a great cost for any black who thought differently. The so-called moral majority could do just what they wanted and not be concerned about breaking the law or receiving retribution for their evil deeds done to black people. This was in the 1950s and '60s and not so long ago. The types of punishment included brutal beatings, castration, branding, and death by hideous methods. (Hangings even occurred in some places in the South.) And often blacks would receive visits from their praying neighbors, but these were no church folk that you would want to meet. I am talking about KKK visitations. These visitors always seemed to have a fascination with fire and crosses. Surprisingly, they called themselves Christians. Even white folks (many of which could be found in the finest Southern churches) who said they were not part of them showed the actions of agreeing with their philosophy and by that supported their actions. Even today, I find it hard to believe that such deceivers will enter the gates.

Everything was separate. Blacks could not go to many of the same stores that whites went to; there were separate bathrooms and water fountains. It was normal to see signs saying, "White Only" and "Colored." Blacks could not sit at the front of buses, and if there were no seats left for the white people, the black people were forced to get out of their seats and stand. We were not allowed to use their swimming pools or visit their parks, even though these were public facilities.

We blacks could not freely express our opinions without repercussions. My parents and grandparents had never voted; blacks had no representation in the political system and faced a dark and gloomy future. So as a little black boy growing up in the South, in the Selma community to be exact, I looked to God on many occasions and sometimes several times a day and asked my God, "My God, my God, why have you forsaken us? I love you, Lord, but why do you love the white people so much more?" I was just a little boy, and after all, that was what we heard from the white South, and most blacks had accepted this to be our fate.

There was much to be afraid of in the South but more to cause anger. I asked my dad so many times, "Why does God like them more than us?"

My dad would always say something like, "Who are you to question God? Just believe in Him and one day, things will change."

Well, you can imagine the next question: "WHEN?"

He would tell me, "I don't know, but I want you to keep believing."

I would then ask, "How will they change?"

He would say, "I don't know, but change is coming one day."

During my early years, JFK was considered a friend of the black man, and when he was assassinated, it devastated our household; even my father cried and said that one of God's children had just gone home. As a little boy, I memorized a saying of JFK: "Ask not what your country can do for you, but what can you do for your country." Around the same time, a young preacher named Martin Luther King Jr. was pushing an agenda that disturbed the greater white South. Dr. King wanted to cash in on the promise of the founding fathers of American freedom.

He became the mouthpiece for us blacks and was determined to make a difference. I can't imagine any place being worse than Selma. We black people didn't have the freedoms of our white counterparts and were still treated like slaves; yes, even in 1965. Dr. Martin Luther King Jr. was our Moses to lead us to the Promised Land.

Dr. King brought us much-needed hope; prior to his time, there was just a deep sense of despair and hopelessness. Truly, we blacks of Selma, Alabama knew something about how the Jews felt in captivity. It was like living in a fertile land, yet we could not taste the fruit. Even though there was great fear, there was great hope also, and everybody knew that something bad had to happen before something good would occur. With the arrival of Dr. Martin Luther King Jr. and the civil rights movement in Selma, Alabama, I could see the words of my father taking root: "Just believe that change is coming."

Klan rallies were on the increase, and the KKK as well as other local whites was turning up the pressure on all of us blacks. I can remember seeing, hearing, and feeling their anger and racial slurs. No one in our family was attacked, but we endured much verbal abuse personally as well as corporally. Several other black people that we knew were beaten and battered, homes were set on fire, cars and trucks were run off the road, and people were driven out of town for no apparent reason other than wanting to share in the same freedoms that was promised to all Americans.

Around the age of five, I remember a dark day known as Bloody Sunday. The date was March 7, 1965. The goal was to stage a march from Selma to Montgomery. This would require the marchers to cross the Edmund Pettus Bridge in Selma. The governor of Alabama was George Wallace, who was one of the biggest racists and segregationists of the South. He gave orders to the local law enforcement to prevent the marchers from crossing the bridge.

So on this day, the eyes of the whole world were on Selma, Alabama. What occurred was shocking to America but not the black community of Selma and surrounding areas. We knew that the hate whites in Selma had for blacks, was much stronger than the love presently offered. As the marchers proceeded, police officers converged on them with no regard to doing them bodily harm. We were not at the bridge but in church in Sardis, just outside Selma. We had an old black-and-white thirteen-inch TV that worked sometimes. This Sunday it worked and we saw the wrath of an angry white south led by the law authorities poured out on a brave group of freedom fighters (blacks, Jews and some whites). We also turned on the radio to hear more bits and pieces of a dream that seemed to be fading away.

I was terrified by what I heard and saw. With the entire family circling the radio and TV as if we were in a prayer service, we watched and listened. We saw many people that we knew being attacked. People were being beaten with clubs and nightsticks and with the butt of shotguns, tear gas was being thrown into the crowd of marchers, powerful water hoses were used to spray the people, and I seem to remember dogs being used as well.

I could see the cuts and wounds of my people and remember asking my father if we could go participate in the march, but he told me that we would just be hurt or killed like the people we were seeing. Some of my older brothers wanted to defy my father, but he told them that if they went that they would never be welcome to return. It's a funny thing to see your people sacrificing for you and not being able to do anything about it. I remember telling my father that I would rather die than live the rest of my life as a slave. At that point, he made me stop watching and told me to get out the house. I was just five years old and I was having great difficulty with what I had just seen and heard.

So I went outside, crying deeply because all my hope of being free had diminished through the strong arm of the white South. I once again asked God, "Why was the black man forsaken?" Little did I know then that the answer to such a question was really in the hands of humanity. Nevertheless, it was one of the most terrifying things to see, and it was in my hometown. I remember wondering how we would ever be free (free meaning equal too). Would we ever have the same rights and freedom as other Americans? Would justice ever be served to those who unfairly and unjustly imposed abuse and terror on my people? I seriously wondered and cried, "Who will save us?"

On that Bloody Sunday, the rest of America got a glimpse at life in Selma and a quick snapshot of the resistance, which we blacks faced on a daily basis. Another march was scheduled for about a week later, and the National Guard was ordered to provide protection. There was some heckling but no physical abuse, and the marchers made it successfully to Montgomery, Alabama.

Even today, I remember Bloody Sunday as if it was yesterday, and I don't suppose that I will ever forget it. For many years, I had a great fear of walking across the Edmund Pettus bridge. When I was in high school, each year during Black History Month (February), there would be a traditional march, but I could never overcome my fears. I dreamed about this bridge at least once a week, every month and year until I passed the age of sixteen.

After turning sixteen years old, I worked in the Yellow Front supermarket. You could view the river and the Edmund Pettus bridge from Yellow Front. I would see it and always feel fear. One day I could find no one willing to give me a lift home after work and it was getting dark. My father refused to come and pick me up, so I started walking. As I got to the tip of the bridge, I was terribly afraid, and all I could think about was Bloody Sunday and falling off the bridge into the river, but I had no choice. It was the only way home. I began to say the twenty-third Psalm. Verse 24, "Yea though I walk through the valley of death, I will fear no evil, for thou art with me, thy rod and thy staff, they comfort me…" was a key verse for me because I was very afraid, but I kept stepping and I kept saying the twenty-third Psalm, verse by verse and step by step. I was crying but still moving forward. After what seemed like a lifetime but in reality were only a few minutes, I noticed that I had crossed over the Edmund Pettus bridge; the Lord and I had crossed over.

I still had about nine miles to go, but I was in much better shape then than now. I began to quote scripture and started trotting, and before I knew it, I was at home. The whole journey had taken two hours.

I still have dreams of the Edmund Pettus bridge and falling off it from time to time, but now it's different. I am no longer a five-year-old oppressed by a white Southern supremacy society but a man of God, blessed by Him and cherish the freedoms of being an American, but more important, I cherish the freedom offered me by Jesus Christ. Many Americans have died and lost much just so their children might have a better life or the opportunity to have a life of liberty and freedom in America. To all my people before me who gave so much, to all the white people, Jewish people, and all others who stepped out of their comfort zone to do what was right, godly, and morally correct, I thank you. Because of them all, America is closer to being a nation that lets freedom ring.

Chapter 3 I Was in Love with Mary Jane

I hated my first, second, and third day of school. Actually, I hated the whole week. The other kids were very mean and picked at me for many reasons. They ridiculed me because we were poor and because of the way that I was dressed. Many of them had parents who despised my father because he had a reputation for having higher standards for his children, which their parents would not enforce. They bugged me because I had a big gap in the front of my mouth caused by a couple of different things, the first of which happened one Sunday afternoon when I was playing in the yard with my brothers and sisters.

One moment I was running, and the next thing I remember was my father shaking me, saying "Wake up!" I had run into the iron swinger in the backyard and knocked myself out. I had a really bad headache and didn't feel like moving. Within a few minutes, I got up and was getting ready to play some more, but I noticed a funny feeling in my mouth. There was no blood, just a strange feeling at the front of my mouth. I had knocked out one and a half teeth from the front of my mouth. Going to the doctor for this was unheard of to my father. He rubbed my head, checked for blood, and said, "You'll be all right."

The second reason is that my father gave me a lot of candy, which didn't help my teeth. Add this to poor dental hygiene and you end up with the nickname "Snaggletooth." That's what all the kids from school called me, all of them except for Mary Jane.

They were not alone; my first-grade teacher was mean and hated me as well. She laughed with the other kids when they made fun of me. Her name was Mrs. Wrong, but she could have been the Wicked Witch of the West in *The Wizard of Oz*. She was one of those blacks who favored blacks who had a lighter skin complexion. You see, in the South, the mind of many blacks had been poisoned by the wounds of a white dominated society, which was free to enforce the injustices of a white-supremacy philosophy. Mrs. Wrong was one of those blacks who thought white was better and that blacks who had a lighter skin complexion were superior to those of us blacks who had a darker skin tone.

You may be asking how this ties in to my love for Mary Jane. Mary Jane Wilson was in my first-grade class with Mrs. Wrong. Mary Jane could be called a light-skinned colored, so without any other explanation or reason, she was the favorite of Mrs. Wrong. Everyone knew that we could not make Mary Jane cry or that all she had to do was look at you and point and Mrs. Wrong was ready to pounce on the poor subject, just like that. Mary Jane was always kind to me. My father had a good relationship with her parents and would sometimes do work for them and I would tag along. I knew her before school, and she had been sweet to me at my mother's funeral. I remember her hugging me and kissing me because that was what everyone else was doing. She held my hand and said that she would be my friend forever. She was a female other than my mother showing me attention different from that of the females in my family, and it felt good.

Mary Jane and I would cut up in Mrs. Wrong's class, but I was the one who got the punishment. During that time, corporal punishment in the schools was perfectly legitimate, so I got several whippings at school, but just so you understand, they were nothing like those that my dad gave. Mrs. Wrong used a twelve-inch ruler to swat across the palm of my hand. One day Mary Jane suggested that we hide in the supply closet so that she could give me a kiss; I was game for it, as I was for anything that Mary Jane wanted to do. I had determined that no matter what the consequences were, I was willing to sacrifice to make Mary Jane happy and be close to her. Mary Jane and I went into the closet, and as she was beginning to kiss me, the door opened and all of the kids laughed. Mrs. Wrong grabbed me by the shoulders, pulled me out of the closet, and began to beat me with the yardstick, really bruising my wrist, arm and shoulder. I cried for the next hour, and then it was time to go home on the bus.

Nothing was done to Mary Jane. Mrs. Wrong told Mary Jane to stop being around me because I wasn't good enough to be around her, but Mary Jane refused. When the bell rang, Mrs. Wrong just looked at me as I walked out the classroom with Mary Jane at my side. She looked at my swollen wrist and tried to soothe me by holding my other hand and with a kiss on the cheek, but not even Mary Jane could make me feel any better.

When my father got home, my sister Geneva told him about it; he was hot but did not punish me again. He asked me what happened and I told him. He then looked at my arm and wrist and saw the swelling. Now that was one thing about my dad: he didn't mind the teacher punishing us, as long as it was done fairly and without injury. He then said that he was going to take me to school the next day. We all knew what that meant; he was not very big or educated, but somehow when he threatened to do something, everyone took it seriously. That was the reputation he had.

He took me to school the next day and asked Mrs. Wrong to step outside for a minute. Mary Jane looked at me and smiled and the world was right again. Mrs. Wrong opened the door and my dad called me, not by my real name but by the nickname, he always called me. "Pop, come out here." He then asked me to repeat what I had told him. While I was telling what happened, Mrs. Wrong interrupted and said that Mary Jane had nothing to do with it; she then called Mary Jane out and asked her to describe what had happened. Before Mary Jane could say anything, my dad asked Mrs. Wrong why she was willing to take Mary Jane's version over mine. He then made the statement that his children were not perfect, but that I was not a liar — that I might talk, too much but was not a liar. She then told him that I had behavior problems. That did it. My dad began to yell at Mrs. Wrong and told her that she didn't have any business trying to teach school because she couldn't be fair to the children. He also told her that she had better not touch me again and that if she had a problem with me that she should contact him. My father used a few more colorful metaphors on Mrs. Wrong that day. She was in tears when she came back into the classroom. The next day she isolated me from the rest of the class and made negative comments toward me for weeks. I told her that I was going to tell my father, and the next day I was moved to another class.

I really missed being in the same class with Mary Jane. We were able to see each other at lunchtime, but it just wasn't the same. Periodically my dad would go to their house for something and I would go with him just to see Mary Jane. Not long afterward, Mary Jane moved, and I never saw her again. I missed her greatly but cherish the memories that she gave me. She never poked fun of me like the other kids and she remained my friend even after Mrs. Wrong told her not to be my friend. She was there when my mother passed on and she will always be special in my book.

Chapter 4 When My Older Siblings Came Back Home

*B*ack then, we didn't know of any black people who had telephones; anytime an emergency would occur, Western Union would be used to get the word out. Under normal circumstances, we sent letters. Some of the happiest memories were when we would receive a letter from one of my older brother or sisters stating that they would be coming home to visit. Christmas was always a good time for them to come, but any time they came was a God-sent blessing. Once we received the letter, my father would automatically perk up and seem happy. We would all be happy to see them because in our minds, they had left this terrible place called the South (except for James, the oldest) and were making a life for themselves somewhere else without being a field worker, maid, or cook. They were busy out there making something of their lives, and this was encouraging to us kids who were still at home.

Knowing that a sibling was returning home meant doing some extra cleanup. We all worked to make the shack of a house look better and more presentable.

None of us was bothered by the extra work; but happily worked in preparing for our big brother or sister. Flying was out of the question; their arrival would be by bus or car (car the majority of the time). Knowing the day of arrival from an earlier letter, we would wait up many nights, just waiting to see a car pull up in the yard. That was the only time my father would let us stay up that late, and then we had to burn a kerosene lantern to keep the electric bill low. We still could not keep the TV on past 8:00 p.m. during this time, so Geneva, Howard, and Sanguretta would tell stories. We would also bake some sweet potatoes in the kitchen stove in the section where we put the wood. We kids would all be around the stove telling stories and entertaining each other without the help of any radio, TV, or electronic equipment.

Finally, we would hear a car drive up, car doors slam, and a knock on the hallway door; they had made it home and the house would be filled with shouts and laughter for hours. Anytime an older sibling would come home, they would always do something special for the house by buying some needed item or clothing for the rest of us and sometimes a favorite toy that we might have wanted but would never have received otherwise. They would also do things that today you might call small, but then, those little things meant the world to us. I would notice my father and see that he would be so proud of them, and when people would come up to him in my older siblings' presence, he would proudly say, "This is my son or daughter from California, or Colorado, or Chicago." Understand that having left the South and living in the previously mentioned places meant something to those black people still living in Selma, Alabama because they had escaped the South.

Seeing them again brought and restored hope for the rest of us kids that we too could and would make it out of the South and, like my older brothers and sisters, return with a good report for the rest of the family. We also knew that while they were visiting, my father would be less likely to whip and punish us. He was always in a better mood, but with him, we knew that if the crime were worthy, we would still pay.

It wasn't all roses with the older siblings when they came home. Once I think we saw a western TV show where someone was hanged. I later attempted to hang one of our puppies on the back porch, but my older brother, Earnest from Chicago, saw me and yelled, "Pop, you are crazy! You'd better stop, put that puppy down, and don't run!" I know that this was a cruel and bad thing to do, but when I was doing this as a little boy of age six, I just really didn't think of how terrible a thing this was. But when I heard my big brother yelling at me, it came to me that I was doing something hideous, dark, and bad. I was able to stop, but knowing that I was probably doing something terribly wrong, I ran. Earnest ran after me. It seemed as if he ran after me for hours, but it was probably more like five minutes; I ran around the house and he was right behind me. Going around the house about the fourth time, I dove under the house in the midst of chicken and dog droppings; this had worked with other siblings, so I tried it with Earnest. Sure enough, Earnest was not able to follow me. He tried desperately to follow me under the house, but he was just a little too big and my determination not to be caught was much greater than his will to punish me. From this, I learned a valuable lesson: when faced with adversity, one must have the willpower to survive and it must exceed the determination and willpower of one's adversary. I stayed under the house for a good hour or so. Eventually Earnest left me alone and had to go with the others to visit some friends or somebody. I felt bad that I had attempted to do this evil deed and even worse that my big brother was angry with me, but most importantly, he didn't mention it to my dad. If he had, I am sure that my dad would have worn my rump out. Later he asked me, "What were you thinking?" I told him that I was doing what I had seen on TV. He then explained to me that TV was not real and that the next time I saw something like that, I should ask someone about it before trying it. To me, this meant that if I had to ask someone, I had better not do it. So after that, I never tried anything like this again (that is, if you don't count throwing rocks at the chickens).

Chapter 5 My Dad – Was it Love or What?

I remember seeing and smelling cotton for as long as I can remember. All of my sisters and brothers picked cotton, but I was spared by the white man's use of the cotton-picker (a tractor that could automatically pick the cotton). That was not the end to hard work. Everyone in the family had a purpose or they didn't eat, even the animals. I remember my dad calling one of our dogs to go and gather the pigs. The dog didn't come, and so my dad got his gun and went looking for the dog. No matter how hard we worked, it would never be enough to get us out of the grip of poverty already determined by the racist South. At least that was what many blacks in the South were led to believe. What made my father different? He didn't buy into that white-supremacy brainwashing. My dad had a sixth-grade education, but he never let that stop him from educating his children.

During these days, blacks had to come to the back door of whites in the South. It was an open understanding; failure to do so could have serious repercussions. I remember following my dad to the farm owner's house, to the back door. Out of nowhere, my dad began to yell at me. I could not understand why until later that night. He told me to never follow him to any white person's back door and that his plans for his children would be to come in through the front door and that we should set our eyes to that day. He went even further by telling me that no matter what happened to him, there were four things that I should always do, no matter what:

- Keep God first
- Maintain loyalty to family
- Be the best at whatever I did
- Leave this place

"Do these things, Pop, and you will never have to come to anybody's back door. I do believe that you can own the house."

For as long as I remember, my father worked hard and did not slight on teaching us kids that principle. He only had a sixth-grade education and had to leave school to help provide for the family. His wisdom and hard work ethic cannot be taught in any school nor hatched at any university. In the area of advice and wisdom, he taught us well. He knew how to communicate with people, whether good or bad; no one ever misunderstood what he meant or stood for.

My father was a sharecropper, meaning that he didn't own the land or the old shack that we lived in but had an understanding to work for the white landowner in return for living on the land. This was a common practice in the South and perhaps still exists to some degree today. It was not uncommon to look out on the landside and see little shacks surrounded by cotton fields or located at the edge of swamplands. Well, our shack was an old wooden shotgun house with a tin roof; many of the barns of the white people around Sardis were in better condition. The only running water we had was when it would rain hard and the rainwater would run down the walls or leak through the tin roof. We had a pump in the front yard, and every day we had to pump water for cooking, bathing, cleaning the house, doing dishes and washing clothes. As mentioned earlier, we had no gas but used a wooden stove and a fireplace when it was cold. On cold nights, we would heat up small irons in the fireplace, and when we went to bed, we would wrap the hot irons up in a blanket and put them under the covers at the foot of our beds. This worked great and kept us warm through the night.

The house was called a shotgun house because it had a hall that separated one large room from the rest of the house. When you looked at the house, you could see straight through the house if the hall doors were open. The room across the hall was called "across the hall." It had a bed, couch, fireplace, and an old piano sold to my father by the white owners. On the other side of the hall, there were three rooms (my father's bedroom, the kids' bedroom, and the kitchen).

My father's bedroom had his bed, my mother's bed (which later became my stepmother's bed), the fireplace, a hand-me-down black-and-white TV, a few chairs, my father's favorite chair, a "shiftrow" (used as a closet to store clothes, shoes, etc. – my father used it to also store a few more guns) and a few shotguns on the wall. The next room had no heat and was a bedroom for all the children (the boys on one side of the room and the girls on the other). The last room was the kitchen, which had no heat other than a wooden stove (in later years, the wooden stove was replaced by a gas stove). In the kitchen, we made glue from cornhusks and corn peelings, which were used with old newspapers to wallpaper the walls. You could look up and see through the top of the house; even view a few stars at night. It was the home of many critters as well. There was no carpet in this shack, just a wooden floor.

What was it like being a poor black family in the South during the '60s? Being poor didn't bother us that much while we were living in it. It seemed to bother other people more because they rubbed it in our faces; the white people were not the only cruel ones, but black people were as well. I could never understand why my own people would be so hard on us because the majority of them were in the same predicament that we were in, except they didn't have Lee Earnest Coker as the head of the family. Even though we were poor, my father pushed us to look beyond the present time. Yes, we were no strangers to poverty, but we never felt poor because my dad stayed on us like white on rice and we never took time out to feel sorry for ourselves. This I think caused many to say that we were trying to be more than what we really were.

There was no inside plumbing, no showers or bathroom sinks, and no dishwasher either. Most importantly, this meant no suitable toilet, and we had to go to the outhouse to use the bathroom. I remember using baking soda and a towel to clean my teeth. Taking a bath meant carrying buckets of water that you had to pump and then carry to the kitchen area (not really a real kitchen) and heat on the stove, which required wood. We had a tin pan called a "foot tub" that we put the bathwater in to take the bath. During winter, we would wash up or take baths in the kitchen area or in one of the rooms that had a fireplace. (Only two other rooms had fireplaces, meaning that the room in which all the children slept had no heat.) Today you can see the foot tub used to hold beer, soft drinks, and ice, but every time I see one, I think about hard times. We never really had a modern bathroom.

We were so poor that we never had normal toiletry or bathroom items. (Toilet paper? What was that? We made our own from whatever we could find.) I never knew toilet paper existed until I went to school; we just used whatever paper we had. I know this sounds hard to believe today, but this was not just a unique experience that the Coker family was having; it was widespread in the South with most black people.

Boy, did we hate the outhouse—heaven forbid when you had to go at night. The safest thing to do was to get someone to go with you, but it was never easy to get a sibling out of bed or to leave the house to walk down to the outhouse. (It was about sixty yards from the house and had no lights leading to the path or in the outhouse itself.) If you had to go during the winter, then you had to face the cold and sometimes the rain, and if you went at night, you had to carry a flashlight. Let me tell you; there were plenty of cold nights in Sardis.

One good thing about going into the outhouse in the winter was that there were no snakes. Any other season but winter, we had to consider the possibility of snakes and lizards. Many times, snakes, lizards, and rats paid us a visit. I vividly remember an encounter one of my sisters had with a snake in the outhouse; it was one of the scariest days of my life. My sister's blood pressure skyrocketed and she was immobile for the rest of the day, and the snake was still on the loose. When my dad got home from his work assignment for the day, he was in a foul mood. (He was in a foul mood most of the time, and it never seemed to take much to set him off.) He fussed at us for my sister being sick and really put us down for not killing the snake. I was thinking that he couldn't mean me; after all, I was only five years old. But it didn't matter. When my father fussed at or punished one of us, it was like punishment for all of us, though not as severe.

So my dad, mad with the world, mad at the white man, mad at his position in life, mad at his children, set out, using many colorful metaphors, to the outhouse to do the snake in. (I felt sorry for the snake.) Within about fifteen minutes, there were all kinds of noises coming from the outhouse. Ten minutes later, my dad left the outhouse with one dead snake. Even to this day, I hate snakes and on the farm, you learned to kill those that posed danger.

Spring break was a good time except for one nasty, disgusting experience that my dad would bestow upon us; it was spring-cleaning, and I don't mean house cleaning. This was the time when my father would give us a big dose of castor oil. He would try to disguise it in a half cup of orange juice or even a little coffee. There was only one other occasion when we would drink orange juice, and that was when we were really sick. So seeing orange juice on spring break meant having to take a big nasty dose of castor oil. The reality was the same with the coffee meaning that we knew when we were given coffee, that it had castor oil in it. It was thick like motor oil and probably tasted like it too. The castor oil was so thick that it would always be left in the cup after drinking the orange juice. The last thing you would want to do was throw up because that would make my dad extremely angry and he would yell at us, threaten to whip us, and make us hold our noses and swallow it with no orange juice. All of the children had to take it at the same time. You may be asking, "What was wrong with that?" Well, castor oil makes you go to the bathroom like crazy, with only a moment's notice. For us, it meant the outhouse, with anywhere from five to eight kids sharing that hole in the ground, all of us trying to use the outhouse within the same day. This was difficult and very embarrassing. (There were bound to be some accidents.) The castor oil also made your stomach hurt and feel weak, but we were expected to continue working around the house.

We also had to take castor oil anytime we told our father that we were sick. You might think that due to the bad experience of castor oil, we would not try to pull the sick prank. Wrong. We tried it anyway to skip going to church and school, to avoid unpleasant experiences. So if the castor oil was supposed to be a deterrent to make us do right, it didn't totally work. Each time we would weigh the cost, but most of the time; the castor oil was the victor.

There was no shortage to the amazing things that my dad did, some good and some not so good. It was told to me by my older sisters and brothers that one day my mother went to the local store and had a dispute with the white man there who owned the store. The owner slapped my mother. My mother was reluctant to tell my father about it, but he found out anyway. I think all of the feelings of being helpless in this white society must have seriously affected my dad. He got his shotgun and went up to that store to kill this man. My father took a shot at the owner who had slapped my mother and only missed because the white farmer that he worked for interfered. That day there were threats from the KKK that they would be coming to burn our family out. For two weeks black families hid in the cornfields, waiting for the KKK to come, but they never came. This story brings tears to my eyes even now because of the great wrongdoing by a prejudiced South, but it also brings tears of joy because my dad was willing to die to protect the honor of my mother.

That's how my dad was. He was a strict and firm punisher to us for any wrongdoing, whether it was done on purpose or accident, it just didn't matter. But he did not want the white man to lay a hand on any of us, and this he made public knowledge to them: "If any of my children do something wrong, you just let me know and I will whip them, not you." I believe the justice system should take a note from his justice because it was always painful, swift, and had a definite meaning to it: don't do it again.

When I was between five and seven years old, quite often I would meet my dad coming home from work at the end of the day and race him home for about one hundred yards. He would always let me win. (At least I think he did.) This was a fun time for me as well as my dad; he would always ask what happened to me if I didn't show up. I believe my dad took more time to try to treat me special because my mother died when I was only four and a half years old. Even before she died, when I was a baby, I slept in my father's bed because she was so sick. (He and my mother had separate beds; I think this was a common thing in the South for poor blacks.) He would give me bottles of milk in the night, keep me warm, and comfort me to sleep. I don't know how I can remember such things, but there must be a reason, so now I have documented it.

For years I slept in my father's bed until a certain event happened that made me grow up; it was nothing inappropriate. One day, close to my eighth birthday, I went to my grandmother's house. It was off the road behind all of the nicer homes of the white families that owned the land. There was no way to get to her shack without passing by the big, luxurious white houses. There was a feeling of white supremacy in the air so thick you could feel it as much as you could feel the humidity on a hot summer day. Even the dogs of the white people appeared to hate us by chasing us all the way to my grandmother's house. It was a daily thing for us to visit our grandmother. We checked up on her, and each day the dogs of the white people would chase us all the way to our grandmother's porch. At that time in the South, no one ever put their dog on a leash, and these dogs patrolled the perimeter. What could we do except sharpen our skills to outrun these dogs each day because there was no one who would call the dogs off. I don't know how many nightmares I had about these dogs chasing me, but I was glad when two of them got killed because that left only one and I figured that, should he ever catch me, I would be able to take him.

On this particular day, I arrived at my grandmother's house and Billy was there. Billy was the grandson of the white owner of the land; his parent's home was one of the homes in front of my grandmother's house. The nickname for my grandmother was Hun, like honey. Hun's house was smaller than our old shack but had a homely touch to it; still no running water, plumbing, gas, phone, or inside toilet, but it felt peaceful there, maybe because of the swamp behind it and the huge trees that surrounded it or even the open pastures around it.

Well, on this particular day, I got there and my grandmother asked me to gather her some wood. So I began to do as I was told and Billy followed me. (He was a few years younger than me. I was about seven and a half years old and he was about five and a half years old). He began to brag about things that he had gotten and I listened and wondered for a second what it must have been like to be white. The only thing that I had that I felt was special was a small two-inch pocketknife that my dad had given me when I was six. I told Billy how special this knife was to me and showed it to him and then we carried the wood inside my grandmother's house. Billy told my grandmother that I pulled a knife out on him. She asked me if it was true and I said no. She then began to search me, but she didn't find the knife. This is because I must have dropped the knife somewhere when bringing in the wood.

After about a half hour, Billy went home. Then Hun and I heard this loud voice yelling and screaming my nickname. "Pop, come here; what have you done?" I came out to the porch and my dad yelled and fussed at me, "Are you damn crazy? What did you pull that knife out on that white boy for?" I tried to get a word in to tell him that I did not pull the knife out on Billy. He began to search me, but could not find the knife. He then told me to give the knife to him or he was going to beat it out of me. My grandmother interceded on my behalf and told him that she couldn't find any knife and that she didn't believe I would do such a thing. For a few minutes, my father was then arguing with my grandmother, but that didn't last long enough. Within a few minutes, my father was giving me one of the all-time worst whippings of my life.

This thrashing was even more painful because I didn't feel as if I deserved it.   I thought that it was very wrong of my dad to take the word of this little lying white boy over his own son; that cut deeper and in places that no switch could ever penetrate, for my dad had struck a nerve in me that would never be repaired. But that's how it was then: whites were always right. After I received my beating, my dad told me to "git on home and never play with white kids again because bad things could happen. I have never had any problem with these white folks and don't want to have any trouble with them."

When I got home, everybody in the house knew what had happened. They all tried to make me feel better, but I couldn't; I just wanted to be somewhere else. I went to bed without dinner and my dad asked me what was wrong, but I dared not tell him. He then told me that he knew that I didn't do what Billy said but that he felt that he had to punish me to prevent there from being any chance of a problem with the white people that he worked and sharecropped for. This did not make me feel any better; in fact, it made me feel sicker. On this day, I decided that it was time for me to stop sleeping in my father's bed, but I didn't tell him until a month later. I no longer would meet my father to race him home again, because that day, the things he said and did to me totally changed the way I felt about him. I still loved him, but I just didn't want to do things with him like before. It was terribly hard for me to do; after all, he had taught us men to be strong, not letting our emotions get the best of us. It was the manly thing to do.

Chapter 6 Give Me Time to Grieve

*N*ot long after my mother's death, many changes occurred. It was open knowledge that my father was seeing other women, one of whom was the same one I had told my mother about earlier. Not long after that, my sister Bobbie died from a bad case of asthma. You are probably thinking that this is very unusual, but in the South many blacks died unnecessarily because of poor healthcare or no care, and many of the doctors would not even treat blacks, even if they could afford to see them. As a result, many blacks died from less complicated ailments. It didn't matter to the white Southern ruling party that black people were dying unnecessarily; it was common to hear many white people say, "The only good nigger is a dead one." It seemed as if death was staying over our house for a long time, but at least Bobbie was free; no more tears of sadness, pain or oppression from Jim Crow laws. Like my mother, she was now free from any pain this world could offer.

Within a year of the death of Bobbie, we kids and my grandmother, Hun, were out in the yard one day in the fall when we noticed my father returning from Kings Landing (a rural area about eight miles west of us). The car was loaded with stuff—a woman and two children. Then I heard Hun say, "I don't believe it; he done went and married her." Just like that, he had tried to go and replace our mother. I am sure that my grandmother, sisters, and brothers knew more than I knew about such things, but what I knew was enough for me to form an opinion of dislike, distrust, disgruntlement and disbelief.

He brought her in and introduced her as our new mother; this didn't go well at all. She was no older than some of my brothers and sisters. How could she be our mother in any sense of the word? My grandmother was ticked and told him that he would never replace her Patsy with this new wife. All the kids joined the cause with my grandmother, but it didn't matter. My dad was the dictator of the Coker clan in Sardis. He argued with Hun a few minutes and told her to go home. Then he told us children that she was our new mother and that we had better act right and treat her with respect or else.

This was another day that my father lost some respect from his children. How could he think that everything would be all right? How could he just forget about our mother so easily? Most importantly, why did he have to say that she was our new mother? The latter statement is what hurt the most. How could he expect us to accept her as our new mother; she was a stranger, someone else. If that's what he wanted, fine, but why did he have to force the issue by telling us that, we had better start treating her as if she was our real mother. Our lives seemed to be moving rapidly in a downward spiral with no bottom in sight. This was a lot to digest, the death of my mother, the death of Bobbie, and now a stepfamily to contend with as a new family. What little bit of nothing that we had was now a little bit less.

We were content having my big sister Geneva and Hun taking care of us, and we didn't need—nor did we want—another mother; especially one that was younger than some of my siblings. This was a lot to digest with no proper warning. But who am I kidding? This was a pill that would have been hard to swallow no matter what we had been told earlier. We had a strong will of resistance and probably got it from the genes of my father, but all blacks in the South had to learn how to resist for survival's sake. Yes, we resisted with all our might and on all fronts because to not resist was to disrespect my mother, Patsy Lee Mosley Coker.

Therefore, on that day we heard our father but took no heed to his warning, because our mother would not be replaced in our minds or in our hearts. His new wife would never take the place of our mother in any form or fashion. How could he expect us to accept his statements? We were not ready to accept our mother's death, especially after having Bobbie's funeral not more than a year earlier. I swore that day that she would never be my mother. I would never call her my mother, and I would wage war on anyone who deemed it necessary to give me another mother.

For some time I prayed, "Oh, God, let this just be a bad dream. Please help me to wake up from this nightmare." I even prayed to God to take her away or take me away. Even after many pinch marks and bites of my siblings and dogs, I was never able to wake up; I was faced with the reality that my father had turned our lives upside down and that he didn't even seem to care that he had done so. He just kept on saying that he did it just for us. I just couldn't understand that because he seemed to be the only true Coker who was happy with the situation.

One time he repeated that he did it just for us, and I said, "She ain't my mother!" That was the wrong thing to say. I was whipped without any mercy and sent to bed without dinner, but I didn't care because the pain inside was much worse than the pain he inflicted outside my body. Inside it felt like knives cutting away, all of them cutting in different directions, and there was no one there to remove the blades. There was no one to take the pain away, so I learned to endure through the pain. Somehow, I think I became immune to the pain inside, and as a result, I became numb to many basic emotions. He made me do special things for my stepmother as part of my punishment, but I prayed to God to help me take my mind somewhere else, to a place where there would be no white people or poor black people. As a result, I was able to endure these changes, but deep inside, I built up a wall of constant resistance. (I would never accept this new family as mine, at least not all of them at once.)

My father's new wife had two children, Rebecca and Willie Lee. Rebecca was the same age as me, but we never had a good relationship; we existed in a house together, but we had our struggles. It was common knowledge that my father was not faithful to my mother and that there were other kids out there who claimed him as their father. Some even insinuated that my stepbrother and sister were really his children. I went to my father and asked him, and as expected, I received a whipping. He whipped me for asking, but later came and told me that he was not the father. Later on, my stepmother also stated that my father was not the father of her children.

Well, there was one thing that I was definitely sure of and that was that Willie Lee was not the son of Patsy Lee; after all, I was the baby boy. It is to my mother, Patsy Lee, too. Therefore, where my father lay his hat would not cause me distress or sadness. I decided that I would live my life no matter what the truth was and that I didn't need to know what his truth was in order to establish my own. I felt relieved when my grandmother said that they were not my father's kids.

We bumped heads with them from the beginning. My stepmother moved things that belonged to my mother and messed with my mother's rose bushes. (My mother loved flowers; roses were her favorite.) This caused us kids to become very hostile toward her, and then her kids joined in it. It was clear: us against them. Surely, we had the victory. When my dad got home, he took her (my stepmother) aside and told her that it was her house now and that we had better get used to it and that he wasn't going to put up with that from us. He also told us that he had raised us better than that.

So now, the reality of it all was that we had lost our mother, our sister, our home and part of our father all within two years and were batting a negative return. There was no mother to teach me God's way and show the love of a mother. There was no mother to tell me that God would take care of me and give me that special touch. There would be no mother interceding for us between my father and his wrath. There would be no father to show compassion and help us grieve for our lost; just a voice shouting, "Get used to it, cause that's the way it is now." It was apparent that we had also lost the battle and could only hope for the future of leaving someday. At this time in my life, I really did hope the saying was true: that time would heal all wounds.

My stepmother favored her kids, but my father showed the children of Patsy Lee no favor. She had no problem standing up for her kids against our father but hardly ever did so for us (Patsy's children). She did direct activities within the home and did cleaning and cooking chores, etc., but still, nothing that reminded us of our dear mother, Sister. Sister would stand up for us and intercede with my dad when she needed to (even if it meant putting herself in harms way), and she would show us love and affection despite her weaknesses and bad days. Sister would pray for her children and taught me the Bible and its meaning. She punished me when I was wrong but rewarded me when I was good, and sometimes she treated me special just because I was her baby boy.

We never talked about my mother to her or my dad. I don't know why; maybe we just didn't want to make the situation any worst. But either way, it just didn't happen, and as a result, I remember what I remember. I don't know if the outcome would have been better if things had been done differently. Even if we had known that my father was going to marry her, we would have still resisted.

The situation in the house was two adults and neither one of them having feelings of compassion for us. My older sisters and brothers were able to deal with this better than I was; they were older and could talk to each other on a higher level. Well, at least we had each other and Hun, our grandmother.

As time passed, we were able to function more as a family. There were still problems; there were many problems, but somehow, we made it. Looking back, there were so many things to be angry about and many scars that never healed properly. In time, I learned to respect my stepmother and even love her as my stepmother, but never did she replace my mother. I don't think she wanted to. I think my father just said those things to force us to love her; he was very overbearing and an authoritarian. This type of power could never force us to love. This was just another distraction to contend with during childhood that would be thrust into all of the other preexisting conditions.

Chapter 7 A Sanctuary Away from Home

*A*t the time when my father remarried, five of my sisters and brothers were already dead (David, a set of twins [unnamed], Amy Lee, who died with child attempting to give birth, and Bobbie). James, Eula, John L., Earnest, and Eugene had already left home and had moved from the Selma area. James was living in Pensacola, Florida; Eula was in Long Beach, California; John L. lived in several locations, but resided more in Colorado; Earnest was living in Chicago; and Eugene had joined Earnest in Chicago.

It was always a joy to hear from them and an even greater delight to hear that they would be coming home to visit us. This left Geneva, Howard, Sanguretta, and me at home with Aunt Rosanna, my grandfather (my dad's father), Isaac (Ike) Coker, and my father. Hun, my mom's mother, lived about a mile away and was at our house enough to claim residency; that is until my father remarried.

After my father remarried, my grandmother didn't come over as much. I believe she was devastated by the remarriage of my father and his attitude toward her and her grandchildren. Despite this, we still spent quite a bit of time with my grandmother. Her home became a safe haven for Geneva, Howard, Sanguretta, and me. Since my father made it clear that our home now belonged to our new stepmother, my grandmother's place became even more special. It was an icon of familiarity, a home that we could still call ours, untainted by outsiders. Not only that, but there were not many places our father would let us go to visit; there were even times when he didn't want us to go to my grandmother's house, but she would not let him get away with keeping her from having time with Patsy's children. She stood up for us, no matter what my father would do or say, and he could do some surprising things, even for him.

My grandmother was much more easygoing than my father was; she didn't whip or punish us like my father, but then she had more time on her hands to be kind. We didn't care about the reason; we just liked being in her presence. We could be kids without the great expectations of my father. She accepted us for the kids that we were and didn't consume herself with a lot of rules and regulations.

My grandmother made wine with berries, muscadine grapes (similar to grapes but more tart), and plums, which she sold to the Shady Grove Methodist Church and to other men. The church used the wine for communion, but the men who bought the wine used it for not-so-holy purposes. Now, we kids bought it for neither communion nor unholy purposes; we would just sip a little bit out on our own. One day we tried to drink too much and wasted it on ourselves. My father was upset with my grandmother and had a big argument with her about it. He threatened to never let us go over to her house again. Since most of the time when he said something, you could count on him sticking to it; we were really scared that he would not change his mind. But my grandmother swore to him that she would make sure that we would never touch her wine again. I don't remember if we ever tried to get into her wine again, but we learned that the wine wasn't worth losing the sanctuary that she provided.

Hun did some strange things also. I remember (before my father remarried) my grandmother bringing us dinner on a Sunday evening. We all sat down, prayed, and began eating. About an hour after dinner, my grandmother made a startling confession. She first asked us how we enjoyed the dinner. We said it was good and that the chicken was especially good. She then said, "Chicken? That wasn't chicken; that was a chicken hawk."

We had eaten a chicken hawk. Eating a chicken hawk didn't concern my dad so much, but where Hun had gotten the chicken hawk from was a bigger concern. After all, they didn't sell chicken hawks in the supermarket, and even if they did, my grandmother couldn't afford to buy it anyway. She didn't shoot it because she didn't have a gun. Now that I look back at this, I think it might have been road kill. My father told her not to bring any more food to us to eat, but she did anyway.

One day my grandmother was feeding a little child that she was keeping for someone. I saw her chew the food, take it out her mouth, and give it to the child. I had a fit and asked her why and how could she do such a thing. She replied, "I don't know what you are worrying about. I did the same thing for you and you haven't died yet." Not long after that, I saw my grandmother cooking for the church. She put a good heap of snuff in her mouth, and a few minutes later she said something to me, and bam, it happened. She had accidentally spit into the food that she was cooking. She didn't miss a beat. Hun kept stirring the pot (as if nothing out the ordinary had occurred). I didn't ask any questions because I didn't want to know what answer she might give me. This really set my mind to thinking about all the food that my grandmother had cooked that I had eaten. Then I thought, *What about the rest of the women in the churches?* They chewed tobacco and dipped snuff as well. *What have we been eating all these years?* Minus the hawk and snuff, I learned a lot from my grandmother about cooking.

She loved to go fishing, and sometimes she would take us kids with her. There were several little creeks within a few miles of her house. She would have us dig up a few worms and put them in a little tin can, grab her fishing poles, and head off to the creeks. We never caught any big fish, just a few small perch. My grandmother would take the scales off, wash them, season, bread them, and deep-fry them hard, guts and all. We ate them with no complaint and looked forward to our next adventure.

My grandmother was a source for family history. I remember her telling me stories of the family that dated back to the early 1800s. She was born in the late 1880s and told us many stories in great detail. Many times, she told us how family members used to jump the broom to get married as part of the wedding ceremony. There were countless stories revealing the ancestral line of my mother, as it traced back to the plantation and Indian customs. My grandmother was part Indian, but she never told me which tribe. I think that this might be why she had such an independent spirit. Now, when I look back, I made a mistake by not recording all the information that she revealed; I just didn't think much of it at that time.

Then there were those not-so-pleasant stories. She had a son named George that just disappeared. No one ever heard from him again. I have his name as my middle name. My grandmother would tell me of stories of interfamily problems, stories of broken homes because fathers were killed by the KKK or just mad white folk and stories of how black women were raped or abused by white men. Many times the women were only teenaged girls.

Hun told me stories of children being taken from their parents and stories of how the white man forced the black men to fight each other and be at odds. Many blacks had problems with alcohol; my grandfather was one. If you were black and grew up in Selma, Alabama, you became accustomed to such stories, but these were my people, my flesh and blood. Very often my grandmother would get choked up and not be able to finish telling the story, but she remained committed to telling the stories, sometimes making three or four attempts to complete one. She would tell us of black people, some family, who were hanged, some in local trees or in unmarked land sites. Many times, we would be walking with our grandmother and she would stop and say, "Your cousin [or your uncle or someone else] is buried here." This would come back to haunt us later on at night when we were walking back home from my grandmother's house.

Perhaps one of the most important things my grandmother provided was a place to come and talk about our mother, her daughter. Our grandmother would talk about my mother and her siblings. She spent a lot of time telling us how important we were to our mother. We needed to hear these things to give us hope and during this time, something to have pride in.

My father never talked about my mother after her death, but my grandmother made it a point to do so. When my father remarried, it seem like he was able to totally erase the past of my mother, but we kids just were not capable of doing such a thing. In my case, I only had a few years to know her, and even now, I fight to keep what memories that I have alive.

Chapter 8 My Stepfamily and Us

I believe that my father felt bad about the incident with Billy and tried to make it up to me by getting me a bicycle for my eighth birthday. I never remember him saying that he was sorry for anything. Bikes were much cheaper then and more affordable than they are now, but still money was hard to come by for such a gift. However, this was easier for him to do than just simply saying, "I'm sorry." Normally, birthdays came and went in our house without any special recognition. This bike really gave me freedom, as I rode it everywhere. My stepmother and others would always ask me to go to the store; other black housewives would ask me to go to the store for them. The store was about two miles from our house, but I didn't mind, because before I had the bike, we would have to walk to the store. Sometimes other mothers would give me a quarter for going to the store for them; a quarter used to buy a lot more then than now. I rode my bicycle to my grandmother's house all the time. The bicycle was extremely helpful when it came to outrunning the dogs on the way to Hun's house. I went to the store for her also.

My stepbrother also got a bike even though it was not his birthday; I think this was more of his mother's doing. Within a year, he had destroyed his bike and would always try to ride my bike. After he rode my bike one time and broke one of the pedals, I saved up enough money to buy a cheap lock to put on my bike. This was the only way to protect it from being destroyed by him. He destroyed many of my things and was never punished for such actions. Often, I would work little odd jobs and sell magazines to buy little toys and science projects that most children got from their parents, but it just seemed that my stepbrother had something inside of him that said, "You can get Calvin's things and do what you want with them."

Earlier he had destroyed my walkie-talkie set, broken my piggy bank, broken my microscope, and destroyed several neat science projects that I had completed. I took pride in these things because they were a sign of my accomplishments and hard work. My father and stepmother never took any strong action to stop this behavior. I could not understand or comprehend their reluctance to introducing him to the same kind of punishment, which my father so graciously shared with my siblings and me. My stepmother would always try to trivialize the damage that Lee had done, and my father would pretend to ignore the whole situation. My anger grew with the passing of each day. Lee and I fought all the time. I remember throwing a bottle at him and hitting him in the head with it. That day my stepmother attempted to whip me, but Sanguretta got involved and tried to stop her. At that time, Rebecca, my stepsister, also joined in. Well, when my father got home, my stepmother told him that Sanguretta and I attacked her. We did our best to explain what had happened, but it didn't matter to him. We got a royal whipping from my dad that night and a queen of tongue-lashing from him. The line had been drawn, but it was a long time before our stepmother tried to lay hands on us again. You may be asking, What's the big deal? My stepmother didn't want my father to whip her children, and that was the double standard of the Coker's home.

When Willie picked a day to be good, which was rare, Rebecca, his sister, had his slack. She was not as destructive as Willie was but lacked the drive of hard work. We all had chores to do every day. The boys were responsible for feeding the animals (pigs, dogs, goats, and chickens), chopping and bringing wood into the house. We also were responsible for keeping enough wood burning in the smokehouse to slowly, cure the pork.

The girls were responsible for helping to keep the house clean, helping to cook, and washing clothes. All of us were responsible for pumping water and carrying it into the house. Sanguretta and I would end up doing a lot of the work that they were supposed to do, and there was no one there to straighten things out. Once again, we would complain, they would accuse us of not doing our part and nothing would be done. Both my father and stepmother knew what was going on, yet they did nothing to correct this unfair behavior. The best we could do was go and complain to our grandmother, Hun, who would listen with compassion and tell us to just do the best we could and that one day it would all pay off.

My stepmother had several brothers and sisters, and both her parents were alive. One of her brothers, Andrew, would stay with us sometimes. This was soon after my stepmother moved into the house. He was not much of a worker and would always be hiding something. There definitely was something dark about him. Even today, I feel rage inside when I think of his perverted mind and acts. He did some things that were just unthinkable during that time; we (my stepbrother, stepsister, and I) were ignorant to sexual predators and child molesters. Andrew was a perverted sexual predator and capitalized on our innocence and ignorance. During those days, no adults would dream of talking about such things to us children; I wish they had. When he did these things to my stepbrother, my stepsister, and me, I never knew that there was something wrong with it, but I always felt funny and uncomfortable.

He would make it seem as if we were playing a game; at that age (between six and eight years of age), I never knew that this was wrong, so foul and filthy. Not only did he violate us, but also he was teaching us how to violate each other. After about two years of this happening, I felt dirty and knew that there was something unclean about this, but who could I talk to? There was no one that I could talk to about this. The next time Andrew tried something, I told him that I was going to tell my dad, and that was enough to make him stop. He knew that if my dad knew that he was doing these things, that my dad would have killed him dead. If I had just known earlier that this was a bad thing, I could have put a stop to it some time ago.

Even today, I have a hard time forgiving him for what he did; those kinds of things can cause many side effects and issues later on in life. I believe that it affects me somewhat, even today, but not as much as it used to in the past. I used to have dreams regularly about being in public places with no clothes on. Now, I am no psychologist, but I believe that those dreams represented some sexual shameful event of my childhood, which caused me to wake up clenching the covers tight. My wife says that I still clench the covers at night. The dreams are no longer an issue, but I have a compulsion to make everything right; everything must be in order. All things must be in their proper place.

I often wonder if my stepmother knew what her brother was doing, and if she did, why she didn't do something to stop it. I sincerely hope she did not know what he was doing, because I would rather think that she would have acted to put a stop to it rather than permitting it to continue to occur. I never told anyone in my family—I just couldn't—but now that I am older, I had to let everyone know. If my writing this will protect some innocent child, then it was worth me telling the world.

My stepmother had another brother named Wilson. He would always ask my father for favors but never with a thought of doing something to help my father or us. I remember my father giving him money to help his family and food from our table and providing transportation to him when going to town (Selma), but when my father needed help, Wilson would never be around or he would disappear right before the work started.

My stepmother's mother would drink sometimes and would say and do some out of the norm things. Whenever we would go back home, she and Wilson would always ask me to buy them a drink. Forget about asking me "how's life"; all they wanted was their next fix. My stepmother's father was a good honorable man who had great wisdom. He always showed kindness and respect to us. It was hard to understand why some of his children were the way that they were.

The interesting observation is that my father treated them better than he treated his own family, but that's how he was. Outsiders would always see the good father, the good friend, etc., but his children had to deal with a much harsher housemaster.

Chapter 9 *Let the Church Say Amen*

For as long as I can remember, we went to church. I'm not talking about those one-to-two-hour services; church was all day Sunday, and preparations were made on Saturday. It didn't matter how hard we worked through the week or on Saturday; it was understood that Sunday was the Lord's day and that the destiny of our family was set to be in church on Sundays. We were Methodist on my mother's side and Baptist on my father's side. We kids joined New Bethany Baptist Church when the time came. My mother and grandmother were members of Shady Grove Methodist AME. My mother and siblings are buried at Shady Grove. Both of these churches were in Sardis, just a few miles outside Selma.

There was no problem with my parents being members of different churches because none of the black churches had service every Sunday; most had service once a month, the more well-to-do twice a month, plus special programs such as anniversaries, revivals, Men's Day, Women's Day, and Choir Day. We would go to Shady Grove and New Bethany on their Sunday and attend all special programs. On the other Sundays, we would visit other churches. Normally a pastor could have two or three churches; some even had four. This meant that the deacons and mothers of the church really ran the church and hired the pastor to preach and do PR for the church.

We were trained to get up early Sunday morning, eat breakfast, and dress for church. We didn't have any fancy clothing, but it was customary in the South to wear your best to the house of God; all the people believed this was a way of giving God your best. Shady Grove AME was only about one and a half miles from our house, but we went to New Bethany Baptist Church more; it was about seven and a half miles from the house.

We all piled into the old beat-up hand-me-down car and went off to church; sometimes my grandmother would go with us. This was not good because she dipped snuff and would always have to sit near a window to spit. No one wanted to sit next to her because sometimes the wind would blow her spit back in the car. We asked our dad before picking her up to tell her not to dip snuff while in the car; even though it was a good idea, he refused because he didn't want us kids thinking we could tell him what to do. He said something like, "Don't you children be trying to tell me what to do. Um a grown man … don't need none children trying to tell me what to do. Don't y'all try doing that no mo'."

One day that all changed, at least with respect to my window-grabbing snuff-dipping grandmother. When she was in the back behind the driver's seat and spit out the window, a strange wind took the snuff spit and spattered in on my father's white, iron-pressed shirt, some of it hitting him in the face. My dad was so mad that he stopped the car, yelled a few ungodly words, and asked my grandmother to get out of the car. We were mid-ways to church in the middle of nowhere, but he didn't care. We begged him to let her get back in so she could go to church with us. After about fifteen minutes, my father told her to get in the car, but to leave her snuff can out, and never dip snuff in his car again. Now my grandmother wasn't silent either during all of this, and she exchanged some words with my dad—no one could get on him like she could—but that Sunday, it was the children who facilitated our motion to get to church.

Sunday school always started at 9:00 a.m. and lasted until 10:30 a.m. We all were in one combined class of adults and children. Since many of the adults could not read, the children would read the verses and the teacher would ask everyone a couple of questions. After Sunday school, we had a break.

All of these country churches were the same: little wooden dwellings and, like the homes of their members, no running water, plumbing, or heating. Later on, when I became a teenager, I do recall the deacons purchasing and installing a heater in the church. Prior to then, when it was cold, we would gather wood for the heater, and if it were summertime, we would set up fans over the church and open all the windows. When the weather was nice, all the children would play in the woods surrounding the church. What a great time this was in New Bethany Baptist Church.

The sound of the woods surrounding the church made a melodic tune that seemed to have a natural blend with the church. It was common to hear the sound of birds singing, the wind blowing through the trees, the sound of crickets and bullfrogs added their tune.

Church would start again around 11:00 a.m. Everyone would come in and be seated while the deacons gathered up to the front and began leading the old country songs. Many of the words were different because there were no hymnals, not that it would have made a difference since most of the people there could not read or were not very good at it. We little kids use to think "A charge to keep I have" was "Hey, Charles, to keep I have." There was a nice white man named Mr. Charles who lived where many of the white people lived in Sardis, and we kids wondered why the church was calling Mr. Charles. But in reality, they were singing what they thought they had heard their parents singing. They continued singing and praying.

The prayers were long and seemed to bring the worst out of us kids. It was customary to get on our knees when someone was praying, so on my knees I went, waiting for these long prayers to end. I went to sleep many times only to be rudely awakened by the church ushers. Quite often, my sleep was broken by the sound of the mothers in the church jumping up and starting their dance and shouting; they always said that they did this because they were happy. Getting happy is another way of saying that the Holy Ghost has come over them. It was like being at an auction. One on the left would start shouting something and get a dance going and then one from the back would start it up, and then from the right and so on.

Next, the pastor would get up, read the twenty-fourth psalm, and render a prayer. The deacons would take up a collection and pray over the offering. The choir would start singing during the collection and pause for prayer after the collection. Once again, the pastor would get up, but this time he would preach. Now back there during those days in this country church, if somebody didn't "get happy" (crying and shouting), the pastor would preach and preach and preach. Maybe that's why somebody always seemed to get happy within the 45-to–65–minute mark. We kids were ready to get happy within the first five minutes, but we didn't count.

After the sermon, the deacons would take up another offering, so there would be more praying and singing. So sometime around 2:00 or 3:00 p.m., church would end for that day. This was when there was no special program; on Sundays when there was a special program, we would be there until 4:00 or 5:00 p.m. On special programs, there would be guest preachers, and they would always seem to preach even longer than the normal pastor did. There would be another special offering for him as well. At the end of church, the women would give out dinner plates to all of the adults. All of the women of the church would bring a box that they had prepared earlier. We would leave our portion at home to eat. The idea was for the women to give plates to all of the visitors, but what seemed to happen was that they gave plates to their favorite people. However, we kids were on the job. We were tasked to identify the visitors and guests and get them plates by my dad. Since he was the Chairman of the deacon board and had a reputation, no one complained. We would dash in the back room, get a few plates, go and deliver them and soon return for more.

I remember one time when Mary Jane and her family came to our church. I stayed awake the whole time. At first, we sat beside each other, but that ended shortly by the help of an usher on her job. I had told Mary Jane that I was going to get her a plate from Mrs. Johnson. Mrs. Johnson made the best fried chicken and potato salad in Sardis. Everyone knew that her dinners were the best; therefore, it would take some planning to get this done.

So when Mrs. Johnson got to church, I immediately went out to help her unload things from her car. She told me that she was going to save me a plate and to help her issue the plate later; that was what I wanted to hear. She was true to her word. I delivered only her plates that Sunday and got the plate she promised me. I can remember the smell of the fried chicken, potato salad, greens, and sweet-potato pie, but I had promised this plate to Mary Jane and had a real problem. If it had been a plate from Mrs. Jackson or Mrs. Wilson, it would not have been a big deal. So as I was pondering what to do, I looked up and saw Mary Jane at the front of the church with some other kids; she saw me looking at her and went outside to meet me on the side of the church. It was there that I gave her my prized possession, a dinner plate from Mrs. Johnson. She kissed me and went back with her family to leave.

Mrs. Johnson saw it all, came outside, and said something like, "I can't believe you gave that plate away to her. That was your plate. Why did you do it?" I told her that Mary Jane was the best friend that I'd had since my mother's death and that I planned to marry her and that the reason I gave her my plate was that I wanted her to have the best dinner from the church. Mrs. Johnson came and hugged me and kissed me and said, "Don't you change now. Stay sweet like that." She then reached in her box, gave me another plate, and said, "Don't give this one away."

There is one church memory that I must share with you. We were in a regular church service and we had my brother Eugene, who was in the army at that time, visiting us. The deacons were collecting an offering, and after the pastor prayed over the offering, he said to my father and the other deacons, "You boys just leave that money right there on the table." We kids looked at our father and saw the wrinkles in his forehead forming; you see, every time my father would get angry, he would form large wrinkles in his forehead that automatically remind you of a bloodhound. So we knew something bad was about to happen. My father replied to the pastor, "Who you calling a boy? My boys are out sitting down out there. Who you think you talking to?" By now, everyone else in church knew something bad was about to happen as well.

The pastor and my dad were exchanging many words, and none of it was the gospel. Our stepmother told us kids to go and get our father; somewhat reluctant, we obeyed, walked up to our dad, and asked him if we could leave. This was not a good thing to do. He told us to get out of the church if we couldn't sit down and be quiet and, if we said something to him again, that he would whip us right there. So we went back to our seats in total solitude.

The pastor really thought that he was smarter than everyone in the church and that he had the right to do what he wanted to do. He told my dad that he was ignorant and an old fool. Now this made my father extremely angry, and I think everybody in the church knew that things had just gotten much worse. We saw our dad reaching in his pocket and saying to the pastor, "You don't call me a fool; I'll cut your throat, right here, ret now." My brother Eugene went up to the front of the church and told my dad that it was time to go. It was heated, but my dad decided that it was time to go.

We left the church that Sunday evening, and it was a couple of months before we went to New Bethany Baptist Church again. I know that my father felt bad about his actions that day, but we kids didn't mind. We were enjoying the pleasures of being backsliders. About two weeks after this bad day in church, my father broke his leg doing sharecropper work. He believed that he broke his leg because of disrespecting the house of the Lord. I watched my father change during these times.

Since my father had broken his leg, he could not whip us while he had the cast on his leg. (The cast went halfway up his thigh.) During this time, he threatened to whip us, and in many cases, he told us to just wait until he got his cast off—that he was going to whip us then. The broken leg didn't stop him from talking, and with him at home all the time, he found much more to complain about and be on our backs about. He eventually healed and, through many conversations with other church leaders and members, returned to church at New Bethany. A few years later, my father and others had issues with the pastor and he was soon replaced with another pastor.

A fact about the church family was that any grownup could discipline the children. This was okay for my dad, and should other church folk ever discipline us Coker kids, we knew that we were going to get it again by my father when we got home. He would tell us, "I'm gonna beat your rump when we get to the house." He would say this no matter who was around. Some people who didn't know him as well as most would say, "He will forget about," or "He's not gonna get you," but they didn't know Lee Earnest Coker. Once he made the statement, you could count on receiving that whipping even on a Sunday. After warning us of the beating we were going to get, he would be very calm and pleasant around the church, but once we turned off the dirt road leading to the church onto Route 41, he would start the tongue-lashing. When we got home, he would tell the unlucky candidate to get out of their church clothes and go get him a good switch. It was not a good idea to get him a switch less than his expectations. Doing so would cause him to go and get one, and he would get two switches and twist them together. I can't express to you the amount of pain and marks left from this twisting and utilization of switches.

He would change his clothes, come outside and whip us, and then go back inside and have dinner. His whippings always occurred outside where there was plenty of room. But there was another factor also; people passing by on the road could see you getting a whipping. Many kids from school asked me, "What were you getting a whipping for?"

Revivals were a special time in the church during those days and you could see the power that pastors had and the respect that was given to them by the congregation. These revivals lasted for a period of two weeks during the summer and marked a time when churches would try to bring in more members. In the Baptist church, it was customary for thirteen-year-olds to be placed on the "mourner's bench" to be saved. Even though Shady Grove was Methodist, they used the mourner's bench also. The first week of the revival was called prayer week. During this time, it was not necessary for the preacher to attend any of the services. The deacons would lead devotion each night of the week, and all of the members that were present would pray.

On the first night of prayer service, the children that were said to be "seeking their soul salvation" were placed on the mourner's bench. The first pew row was designated for salvation seekers. These children were expected to be doing serious fasting and praying and trying to find God during this period. They were expected to stay on the mourner's bench until they found their salvation. When they found their salvation, it was expected of them to give a dynamic testimony, which included some miraculous event. Some people earlier stated such claims as, "I heard the Lord call me and say, 'it's time to get off the mourner's bench,'" "I saw the Lord descending from the sky," "I saw the angels in the clouds," "I saw my dead grandfather," "I saw heaven open up," "I saw hell open up," etc. I often worried what I was going to do when my time came because my mother had taught me different; I already knew God.

During the second week of the revival, the preaching would start. Different families would have to host the evangelist during his stay; in many cases, the church provided a motel room for the evangelist in Selma, transportation and food. I remember when it was our time to host the evangelist. We had to clean up the shack to the best of our ability. It was very hard to satisfy my father; the bottom line is that it really was a shack and there was only so much could be done. That wasn't the main issue: the preacher had to get the best of the food, the best of the collard greens and ham hocks, the best of the Kool-Aid, the best of the squash and tomato, the best of the cornbread, sweet potato pie, or peach cobbler and fried chicken. (All of these items were produced on the farm by us, but what we could eat was limited.) This was common in the South for poor black people in poor black churches.

Whoever said that eating off the floor is bad for you? I remember being asked to help in the kitchen to prepare food for the preacher. I loved fried chicken, on this particular day, more than the thought of being thrashed by my dad. I purposely dropped the chicken on the floor, and when I attempted to pick it up, I dropped it again; it was a breast, a wing, and a leg. My sister told me to put it away and we would have to eat it for dinner, but when she went out, I bit into the leg, and by the time she came back in and grabbed me, I had finished the leg and had started on the wing. I know this was stupid, but I was a little boy with a big appetite for good old home-fried chicken. My sister didn't whip me because she didn't want to make a scene with the evangelist in the house. I was counting on that—being saved by the preacher man—but mercy only lasted for so long before the deacon, Lee Earnest Coker, brought justice home. He beat me with a peach switch this time, and the preacher said nothing once he found out it was linked to him having to eat fewer chicken parts; preachers really like chicken. Well, I am much older now, but I still love fried chicken, but now I can have the best piece every now and then.

It was evident to my father that I already knew Jesus Christ, yet he insisted that I go on the mourner's bench on my thirteenth birthday. My stepsister was born the same year that I was; therefore, she went on the mourner's bench at the same time. I tried to reason with my dad, but he told me that if he didn't put me on the mourner's bench, my stepmother would get upset and not want to put my stepsister on the mourner's bench. I told him that accepting Christ was a personal experience and that it should not depend on what others did. He had no answer, so he told me to shut up and get ready to get on the mourner's bench.

Well, get ready is what I did. From different little jobs that I did, I bought cookies, drinks, sardines, and crackers. I went through the swampy woods behind our old house searching for the right place to set up camp for seclusion to find God. I found a shady spot near a small creek about a half mile into the woods. It was a very good spot until I saw my stepsister coming toward me from a distance. I then packed up all my goodies and went in the opposite direction. I found another location not as good as the previous one: no creek, but bugs and other little creatures were everywhere. I had no problem sharing with them because I knew they could keep a secret.

While out there in the woods, I wondered how long I should stay on the mourner's bench or what story should I come up with for a church stomping testimony. So I prayed to God to help me know what to say when the time would come. I didn't hear any deep voice coming to me or any signs or wonders.

Around Thursday of prayer week, I really began to feel guilty, not about not seeking God, because how can you find what is not lost? However, I felt guilty because my father thought I was praying and fasting according to what others had done. Somehow I felt that God didn't like what I was doing. You might think that I told my father about it, but you are mistaken; that would have been body suicide. Instead I decided to tell him that Friday that I was ready to come off the mourner's bench. Friday, when I went out "in the wilderness," I took no food. I went out, prayed, slept, prayed, slept, and prayed some more.

When we were getting ready to go to church that Friday night, I told my dad that I was ready to come off the mourner's bench, that I knew God and believed in Jesus Christ as my savior. I told him about what my real mother had taught me when I was little and how it had stuck with me. He then asked me, "If you knew God all this time, why do you get into trouble so much?" That question really shocked me, considering how much my dad did wrong. Well, my answer was that "I don't know why I get into so much trouble, but I believe in God and believe that he has a lot of work for me to do."

He then asked me the question that I expected: "What did you see?" This question I was ready for, and I said that the Bible does not say you have to see something to receive Jesus Christ; just believe and He would do the rest. I read the Bible to my father, and he listened to the reading of the Word. This was nothing new. Often he would listen to us read the Bible, but what was different was that I was linking what I was saying to the reading of a passage in the Bible. He really didn't say much, just "Get in the car; let's go."

When we got to church, I didn't come off the mourner's bench. I kept my mouth closed and was just an observer. I wondered to God how I was going to get through this. Toward the end of the prayer meeting, the mourner's bench was queried, and two kids stood and said that they had found the Lord. I listened as these kids fabricated their experience to please the people with a miracle to justify their receiving God's salvation. They were the same stories that you heard the previous year and the year before. When would the truth be made known?

Sunday, after church, my father told me that he wanted to talk to me. He told me that he felt that it would be wrong to keep me on the mourner's bench and that it was up to me to stay on there or come off. That Monday night came, and when they queried the bench, I stood. The preacher came to me and asked, "What is your testimony?" I said that the blood of Jesus saved me and that the love of God is changing me. Then I could see and hear some of the deacons saying, "He didn't see anything." Then, out of nowhere, my dad said, "There's nothing in the Bible that says you have to see a miracle to be saved. God gave us Jesus and He is always available for us; we just have to trust and believe in Him." I was quite shocked. I thought that my dad had discredited our earlier conversation, but I learned that he prayed on it for direction. He knew that this was going to cause some problems with some of the church folks, but he didn't care; when it came to God, he would do what he thought was right.

Some people said he only did it because I was his son. He then replied, "Many of you and your children have given bad testimonies and your children. And why? Cause you didn't understand." The majority favored my dad, and that night all the kids came off the mourner's bench and not one gave a false, miraculous testimony. That night we all became candidates for baptism, and I said goodbye to the mourner's bench.

My father and stepmother would always go to revivals at other churches. We kids did not have to go. We would wait until they left and go and get corn and watermelons from the fields. We worked those fields; it was only fitting and proper that we sample the fruits of our labor. We would wait until they were well out of sight and then we would all take a task to get the meal ready.

Someone would get the water boiling while one of us went to get the corn. The person getting the corn had to do it without leaving any trace that the cornfield has been disturbed; they must move toward the middle of the field, getting an ear here and there and covering up all tracks. Going to get the watermelon required a special skill; the picker had to thump the watermelon the right way and listen for the ripe sound. We had to make sure that we didn't get a watermelon that was too big because that would leave evidence for my father. All this was done within an hour. It took us about half an hour to eat the corn and watermelon; then we spent the next half hour cleaning up. We buried the watermelon rinds and corn remains in a hole near the house and tried to make it look normal.

It was always safer to eat outside because it was easier to clean up and leave no evidence of our actions. It seemed that my father always knew; sometimes right away and sometimes later. When it was right away, he whipped us after getting in from church and that was it. That was best because we knew he would be tired after a hard day's work and getting in from church. On those days when it was later, my dad would know and ask us if we did it. Now this was a very dangerous question; we knew that he knew what we had done, but he asked anyway. If we said, "Yah-sur, we did," we would be punished more severely because, to him, we had done it without any fear. So we had to make him think that we were terrified of the punishment that he would give us; therefore, we lied and said, "Nall-sur, we didn't do it"; all except for Willie, my stepbrother, who would say, "They did it, not me." He would get just a brush of punishment, while we, Patsy's kids, got the full tongue-lashing and switch treatment.

We knew that we were going to be punished, but the food was good and it was worth trying to see if we could do something and get away with it behind my father's back. You see, the thing is, we knew that our father was going to thrash us today, tomorrow, or the next day. No matter what, we knew that it was coming. So we decided to enjoy and feast when we had the opportunity because living with our father meant living with his punishment.

Chapter 10 Pop, the Barber

When I was a little boy, I had a great curiosity that preceded pain and embarrassment. I was always fascinated with my father's hair clippers and amazed at how the motion of moving an object across someone's head could change their appearance so drastically. My father only knew one haircut, and that was the "bucket rim." This style was to cut all hair off the sides and back and leave just an imprint of hair across the top. My father had the same view of his hair clippers as he did of his guns, and even though we had great curiosity, we knew that we should never touch my father's guns (which hung on the wall beside his bed) or his hair clippers.

At some point in time, before I had fully developed this concept, I decided to give myself a haircut. I had decided that I would do a different cut than the old traditional "bucket rim." I turned the clippers on, and right away, I noticed that they moved in my hand. This made me nervous, but not enough to stop. It was that good nervous—you know, like you are about to do something that you have been waiting to do for years and your payday is here. Well, I took the clippers and took one swift swipe down the front of my head, and that was when Geneva, one of my older sisters, saw me. I imagine that she wanted to laugh and protect me at the same time. Not long after that, my father came in and said, "What the hell have you done? Nobody help him to cut it; you want to look like a monkey, then you just look like a monkey. You gonna go to school just like that."

My father made me feel very small and insignificant. He made all kinds of jokes around me and teased me every time he had a chance. I was glad to go to school because I knew he would not be there. I received great ridicule at school from everyone—little kids, big kids, high-school students. (We all went to Shiloh High School, the school for black children in Sardis, Alabama, at the time.) Even the teachers made jokes and teased me. I could do nothing and could not even count on receiving mercy from my father this time. This was painful, but I learned something from this: that the fulfillment of curiosity always has some reward and that not every reward is positive. In this case, it was a negative reward, but not enough to stop me from being a curious boy; it just taught me to be a little more selective the next time. One thing about people laughing at you is that it is not long before someone else does something just as stupid. This means that the joking, teasing, and taunting only lasted for about three or four days. After that, the joke was on someone else; yes, someone else would be the center of attention. So here I tell you: learn to have patience and longsuffering, and whatever your most embarrassing or painful moment is, it too shall pass. Quite often, you just have to learn to ride it out and believe that one day, a new day is coming that will be different and someone else will be the focus of ridicule or uncensored humor.

Chapter 11 A Swamp Experience

---

*W*hen I was little, I loved to go into the swamp with my father to get wood for the house. Before we got propane in the house, wood was our source of energy for heating and cooking. The back swamps of Alabama were very peaceful and there seemed to be a communication there between all the elements of God's creations. Those of you that have been there know the joy in hearing the water run down the creek as it rushes past the rocks and tree branches in its path or the sound made by the wind as it whizzes by and through the trees, or the sound of birds singing and chanting to one another. There was the sound of bullfrogs calling or the sound of a flock of birds changing direction all simultaneously. There were also sounds heard that I didn't recognize, but they fit in to help create a place that was special and ready for exploring.

There was occasionally the sound of deer running through the woods or even a bobcat every now and then. There were snakes crawling, bugs flying, frogs hopping, all adding base to an already perfect tune. No hate there, no racial discrimination, no poor or rich; just beauty the way God intended it to be.

Even though my relationship with God at this time was premature, I felt and knew that there was something special about these types of places. Deep in my soul, it was as if I could hear a musical masterpiece at work. The shining of the sun, fresh air, and everything else that existed in these swamps played a part in this orchestra. My father probably took us for company and was constantly telling us, "Stay in my sight or something bad might get you."

He would tell us that we had better watch out for "coachwhips." According to him, the coachwhip was a big black snake that had a white ring around its neck and they always traveled in pairs. The idea was that they would chase you down. One would tie you down and hold you while the other would whip you; hence the name "coachwhip." As stated earlier, there was more curiosity than fear. So quite often, we (Sanguretta and me) would set off to find the coachwhip, but we never did; we were always interrupted by the yells of my father calling us.

My father would always borrow the truck belonging to Mr. Bob White (the owner that my father sharecropped for) to go get wood. It was a big red truck with high sides on it. It reminded me of my little red wagon, just a lot bigger. One day my father took Sanguretta and me to the swamps with him, and when we were in the process of loading wood onto the truck, my father said, "Go bring me some water." So Sanguretta and I raced to the truck to get the water. Sanguretta grabbed the water before me and slammed the truck door. After a second, she noticed that I was no longer running after her. My hand was still caught in the door. It took me a good second or two to let out one of the biggest cries of my entire life. At this time, the tranquility of the swamp was interrupted by the screams of a child in agony. As I looked at my hand caught in between the door, I felt dizzy and weak in the legs. I heard no birds, no trees; I heard nothing except the footsteps of my father rushing toward me. I was crying, Sanguretta was crying, and my dad was yelling. In the back of my mind, I was hoping that he didn't have to use the power saw to cut my hand off.

He pulled on the door, but it would not open. He then got a piece of iron from the other side of the truck, put it in near the place where my hand was caught, and told me and Sanguretta to "stop crying 'fore I give you something to cry about." (We cried even more because he was yelling.) What seemed like a lifetime but was only a few minutes finally ended; my hand was free. It was swollen badly and hurt to the touch. My dad took some ice out of the water jar, put it in his handkerchief, and told Sanguretta to hold it on my hand. He then put a big piece of chewing tobacco in his mouth and began to chew it feverishly. This was so amazing to me that I mostly stopped crying. What he did next surprised both Sanguretta and me. He grabbed my hand and spit the entire mouth full of tobacco and tobacco juice on my wounded hand. A few of my fingernails had been broken and were bleeding, but after seeing the mass covering of black substance on my hand, including the blood, I stopped crying from the shock of it all. My hand was then wrapped with his handkerchief and the tobacco mixture.

My dad looked at us with anger and told us to sit on a nearby wooden tree stump and not to move. He went back to cutting up wood for the house, and within a few minutes, the birds began to sing again, the frogs were humming, and the deer were moving. The disturbance that we had caused had been absorbed by this wonderful place, and things were already back to normal in the swamp. I, in return, had a very sore hand for a few weeks but was ready to go back to the swamp the next time that my dad went. I think he knew how much I liked being in the swamps, so he let me go. He just warned me that if I got my hand caught in the door again, he might have to cut it off with the chainsaw.

Chapter 12 1, 2, 3 ... 10

Sanguretta was the baby girl and was four years older than me. My dad called her Sandfoot. I'm not sure why. Sanguretta and Howard (next in age, two years older than Sanguretta) normally hung out together, but occasionally she and I would hang out together. When I was five, I remember playing a game with Sanguretta. Sanguretta had this big peppermint stick and knew I wanted some of it, but she refused to share it. She told me that if I could count to ten, she would give it to me. Earlier she had heard me having difficulty trying to count, but what she didn't know was that I had been working on it all day.

So I began to count, "One, two, three, three and a half ... four, five... five and a half." Then I started over, "One, two, and three, three and a half ... four, five ... five and a half, six, seven, seven and a half...." One more time I started over, "One, two, and three, three and a half ... four, five ... five and a half, six, seven, seven and a half, eight, nine ... nine and a half, ten." I then asked for the peppermint stick, but she opened it and started licking the top of it. I went through the house crying. Geneva, my big sister, who was two years older than Howard and was the sibling in charge after our mother died, caught Sanguretta, took the candy stick from her, and gave it to me. I stopped crying, but Sanguretta started. About twenty minutes passed and my grandmother showed up and said that she had heard my sister crying all the way over to her house, which was about a mile away. She gave Sanguretta a piece of candy, but that didn't take care of the problem. Sanguretta tried to get me to play another game, but I refused, so she tried to take the big peppermint stick, but Geneva put her to work and told her that she was going to tell our father if she kept it up; during the next few hours, there was peace in the house.

Chapter 13 Tasting the Sauce

---

*A*s stated earlier, our grandfather, Ike Coker, was an alcoholic. Howard and Sanguretta always wanted to sample his alcohol, but they could only do that and get away with it if everyone was guilty. So they would wait until our stepmother was occupied and then would go and steal some of my grandfather's whiskey while he would be sleeping off a hangover. They had no problem getting my stepbrother and stepsister to wet their lips, but I would always prove to be a bit of a problem. You see, I was a talker; like a man on truth serum, I would spill the beans; after all, "The truth will set you free." Well, I learned at an early age that wasn't all the truth will do. They all knew that they had to get me guilty of the same crime to keep me from talking because I would surely tell. I was labeled to be a "tattle teller," meaning I talked all the time; no secret was safe with me.

I would tell them that it was wrong to do that, that they should not do it, and that I was going to have to tell if they did. This was the only time my sibling plotted with my stepbrother and stepsister against me. They would all chase me down and force some of the whiskey down my throat to prevent me from talking, and this worked until we grew out of that stage. None of them wanted to drink much of it. They just wanted to see what was so good about this nasty stuff that some grown folk seemed to like so much. It was so funny. No sooner did it hit their lips than they were swaying and stumbling as if they were possessed by the bottle.

My grandfather would often bribe Howard to drive him to the store to get a drink. Money was so hard to come by that Howard would do it, even if it meant risking beatings from my dad; after all, we all knew that we were going to get it eventually anyway. Howard could always say that he was just obeying our grandfather, but that was a very weak defense. Many times people would tell us that our grandfather was drunk in the road and we would have to go and get him. I am surprised that a car or a truck never struck him. On the average, we pulled him out of the road at least once a week. I don't mean on the edges of the road but right smack on the yellow divider line.

My grandfather was a kind man, much different from my dad (his son). We grew up not seeing much mercy from our father, but "Cus'n Ike" (that's what we called him) had a kind heart toward us and would give us a nickel or dime when he had it. You see, that was the thing: he normally spent all his money on alcohol.

We kids knew when he would receive a check and would wait for that time to hit him up. Unfortunately most of the time he would spend his check before coming home, and when he got home, he would be drunk. When he went to sleep, we would collect any coin that dropped from his pockets. You are probably thinking that was bad of us, but the fact is that he was throwing away what little he had anyway.

My grandfather became extremely ill when I was eight; he had destroyed his liver and kidneys with alcohol. The doctors recommended that he should be put in the nursing home; back then, that was a way of providing hospice care. Our father didn't like that and had him moved to the house; my dad believed in taking care of the elderly members of the family and did not like the idea of putting any family member in a nursing home. This really wore on the family because everyone had to help take care of him because he couldn't do anything for himself.

A few months later, my grandfather died and was buried at the New Bethany Baptist Church graveyard. We kids thought of all the memories that we had of Cus'n Ike—of how we begged him for change and waited on his unconscious contributions or the many times he asked Howard to drive him to the store, or the times that we got him out of the road. But mostly we remembered him for his kindness toward us kids and how he would always say to my dad, "Lee Earnest, leave them children alone. They all right."

Chapter 14 One Good Deed Deserves Another

We always had chores to complete after school. One day Howard and I were gathering wood from the woodpile and moving it to the porch for the night. We had to cut up blocks of wood and gather chips for the fireplace during the winter months so that we would have some heat in the house. The wood would then be loaded in the wheelbarrow and moved to the back porch and fireplace. We were pushing the third load, and the wheelbarrow was heading straight for the old Ford station wagon. It went straight into it. The damage was one broken taillight. You might think this to be a small thing and perhaps a very insignificant thing, but you didn't know our father. Great fear came over us as we picked up all the wood and moved it to its proper place.

We spoke to our stepmother about it, but she just said, "I ain't in it." Therefore, we were on our own trying to figure out what to do about our dilemma. We went and inspected the damage; the car was old and had several dents already, but we had accidentally broken a rear light. We picked up the pieces and glued them back together, stuck the light back on the car, had Sanguretta inspect it, and were satisfied. When my father was on his way home, we heard him yelling, "Get me a switch, Pop and Howard; go git me a switch, both of you." We tried to explain that it was just an accident, but he didn't care. He told us, "I don't care what kind of dent it was. Accidents still costs." Howard must have known that we were going to get it because he had put on extra pants. My father made us strip to our underwear outside in the backyard, where we could be seen by others, in the wintertime. He then whipped us with those switches out in the open for all public humiliation.

We wondered who had told him about this and then we heard him telling Gertrude that Annie Mae, a neighbor, had told him that we broke the backlight in the car. Why didn't she tell him the rest—that we were busy doing our chores and accidentally pushed the wheelbarrow into the back of the car? Why didn't she tell him that we were not playing—that we were just about finished with our chores? This could only mean one thing: if we ever got the chance, we would get even with her.

About a month later, we saw some strange people at her house during the time that she was at work. For a good neighbor, we would have gone to other neighbors and told them what was happening, but instead, we passed by her house, spoke to the people who were stealing her goods and kept going. Later on that night, my father told us that she had been robbed in broad daylight and asked if we had seen anything strange. We then took a moment to pondered on Annie Mae's description of the events concerning the incident of the broken taillight and replied with a bold face to our dad, "Nau-Sur, we ain't seen nut-thang." This was one day that we felt justice had been served.

Chapter 15 Emergency Room at Shiloh High School

For as long as I can remember, my brother Howard has always wanted to be a doctor. He was sick often because he was diabetic, compounded by the fact that my father wasn't an understanding man when it came to being sick. Kids were cruel also and made jokes of everything, including the sicknesses of others. So it was very difficult for all of us, but especially Howard; regardless of the circumstances, he kept the dream of becoming a doctor.

One day at Shiloh High School, I remember seeing a bunch of high school kids running after a dog that hung around the school for scraps. The dog belonged to Mr. Walker, who was the janitor for the school. Howard was leading kids from his science class in hopes of catching the dog and performing surgery on him. Shiloh High School had a forest of trees behind it, and that was where the dog went, being chased by kids ready to operate. This was all witnessed around lunchtime, and nothing else was heard of this until the next day.

Everybody was talking about how Howard led the group toward operating on the dog. We didn't see the dog for another week, and it was obvious that something had happened to Mr. Walker's dog. When we did see him, he was limping on three legs like an old man with arthritis. From that day on when someone would see that dog, they would burst out in laughter talking about how Dr. Coker performed surgery.

Chapter 16 The Day We Wanted to Swim

On one hot summer day, we had finished working in the fields and there were other children from the neighborhood playing stickball (baseball with a stick instead of a bat) with us. It was so hot and humid that we decided to dig a swimming pool in the backyard. None of the black people in Sardis had pools or even access to swimming pools unless it was a job cleaning the pools for white people. There was a community pool a couple of miles from our house across the street from the Southern Baptist church, which was white outside and white inside too (no blacks allowed). This pool was for the good white folks of Sardis/Selma only. We had heard stories of how many black kids had been severely beaten attempting to take a swim in that pool. There must have been about ten of us digging the hole. My stepmother told us that we were going to get in trouble, and we should have known that this would be trouble anyway, but we kept on digging. We dug this pool about five feet by four feet and three feet deep. We then began to fill it with water. This was not an easy job because there was no water hose and no running water either.

We carried the water about fifty yards from the pump in the front to the hole we had dug in the back. As we added water into our pool, we noticed that it just didn't have that blue pool color. We thought that even if it didn't look blue, it might take a greenish color similar to the water that we saw in nearby creeks, but it was not so. After putting buckets and buckets and buckets of water in our pool, all we had was a mud hole.

We then started the process of scooping the water out of the hole. Soon after, we heard the voice of Lee Earnest Coker rumbling in the valley; at that time, I could relate to how Adam must have felt when he heard the voice of God calling his name in the Garden of Eden. I can also only imagine what Jesus must have felt when he saw the disciples scattering when he was taken into custody; at the sound of my father's voice, every one of my friends who were helping with my pool project scattered like cockroaches when a light is turned on.

Only my stepbrother and I were left holding the bag. My father told us that he was going to whip us but that first we had better fill the hole up with the same dirt that we took out. This was impossible; even if we had not put water in the hole or wet the dirt that we took out, there was just no way this could be done. There was more bad news to come; it started raining. For any of you that have lived in the South, you know that when I say that it rained, that's what I really mean—none of that Arizona skip-hopping rain. It was pouring down. We ran to the porch, but my dad told us to go back out there and finish filling up that hole.

So we went under the supervision of my father and continued to dump shovels of dirt back in the hole. How nice it would have been if there were some big rocks within our path, but Alabama was known for its deep, rich, black soil. We stayed out there for about another hour in the rain until my father heard the powerful sound of thunder. It stormed that night, and that was the only reason my dad didn't whip us. He told us that there was no dinner for us, but I was so tired and exhausted that I didn't care. We slept on a blanket on the floor that night because we were all smelly and muddy. There was not enough water in the house for us to take a bath, and the storm would not allow us to go outside and pump more water.

My dad woke us up at 5:00 a.m. and told us that since we liked digging so much, he wanted us to fill the hole we had made and go help a neighbor dig postholes. It was a long day, and the next day was planned to be a sunup to sundown day, meaning that we would be in the fields from sunrise to sunset. That was the last time we ever dug a swimming pool.

Chapter 17 The Heart of an Athlete

From the time that I was big enough to throw rocks at chickens, I liked sports. Sometimes my father would bring leftover balls from the white folks for us to play with. Occasionally he would see us kids playing catch when he got off work and would come and say, "Pop, throw me a few." He would always tell me that I could be another Willie Mays and that I threw hard for my age. Baseball was really the only sport that he liked. We could only have playtime if all our chores and homework had been completed. There were plenty of times when he ran other kids home and chastised us for not doing things in the proper order. I was very competitive and hated to lose and would dive, slide, and run over, into, or around to score. I was about the fastest in my neighborhood, so I had a reputation for stealing bases. Baseball was fun but really wasn't my most favorite sport, that would have been a tossup between football and basketball, but favoring football.

When it was football season, we boys in the neighborhood would do our chores and homework ASAP, putting dinner off to get an hour of football in. Eddie Mac would bring his football over, and we would play, even when it rained. I was not very big, but learned that speed, when used at the right time and in the right way, can have precedence over size. We played tackle with no pads or gear, just the grass to cushion the blows. We all took turns at being quarterback and wide receiver, but my speed really paid off during these games, and no one could catch me in the open field. It was the same way with basketball. I was short, but because of my quickness, I was able to be a competitor.

I remember looking in magazines in the library and seeing how kids could sell stuff and get prizes such as baseball gloves, bats, balls, footballs, football tees, basketballs, and goals. Even though I worked in the fields, I would make plans on how to buy these sports items. I even took jobs cutting the grass for many of the white people, which really took a lot of time and did not pay very well. I don't know if you have ever seen these huge fields in front or back of the white people's houses in the South, but it would take me about five or six hours to do a job and I would only get five or six dollars. (There would always be another task that they wanted you to do that was not included in the six-dollar deal.) You may be asking why I didn't cut the lawn of black people? That is because all black people took care of their own and didn't have money to pay someone else to do their yards. I went to the store for people and got paid a quarter or fifty cents to build up my bank for the purchase of those sports items.

No sooner did I get these items, when other boys would show up to play. I even remember a couple of boys showing up thinking that they would take over. They were mistaken; we ran them out of the neighborhood. I was always determined to get sports balls and gadgets to try because my heart was into sports.

As my popularity grew, being a sportsman, I asked my father several times if I could participate in sport teams in school, and the answer was always no. He felt that my studying would suffer, but I was persistent; I guess I asked him one too many times. One day when I got home from school, the basketball goal had been cut down. This was dramatic for me. I asked Gertrude, my stepmother, what had happened, and she just said that I should talk to my father about it. Well, after that, I could not talk to anyone or even eat for that matter.

When my father came home, he yelled out why he did it and told me, "You love that damn ball too much; you need to do more with your studying." I thought to myself, *I am an A student. What else can I do?* I then just burst out in tears, and that made him even angrier. He yelled to me, "You too weak. You betta stop that damn crying 'fore I give you something to cry 'bout." But I could not stop. All I could do was see my dreams disappear and think about all the hard work that had gone into my saving and working to get the goal, backboard, and pole. My father then said, "What kind of man you gonna be?" and walked away.

Other kids came over and saw the destruction that my father had done and probably told their parents about it, and from that day on the majority of them stopped coming over. As some time passed by, I believe one of my older brothers, Earnest (we all called him Bay Brother), told my dad that he shouldn't have done that and that it was healthy for boys to want to do what I wanted to do. My father never apologized for doing this, to tell you the truth, I don't really remember him apologizing for anything, but he did tell me that I could get another basketball goal and set it up.

I really had lost most of my ambition to raise and come up with money for sporting items after enduring what he had done. A couple of my cousins said that they would help me put the goal up on the side of an old pecan tree that we had behind and away from the house next to the cotton field behind the house. So we did this, and all of the anger I had against my father came up again. After they left, I stayed out shooting for a couple of hours until someone called me to come inside out of the darkness. I made it a regular practice of shooting for hours, even in the dark.

Now I found myself having the heart of an athlete, not because I wanted to but because I had to. Even though I would never be allowed to play on any team, I would practice as if I were a star, never satisfied but always thinking of the game-winning scenario (three shots, four shots, even five shots in a row from more than twenty feet out) so that I might (within my own mind) be the great athlete.

Chapter 18 Summer Days

Working from sunrise to sunset was a normal occurrence during the summer. This is how we earned money to buy a few clothes, school supplies, and certain household items. The crop that made the most money was cucumbers. Every kid I knew who had to pick cucumbers hated doing it. It was hot and humid and required long hours. My father must have planted around an acre or more of cucumbers. The goal was to start at first sunlight to get a jump on the heat. The rows were long and straight. We would pick the cucumbers and place them in a five-gallon bucket, which we carried as we inched up the row, picking. The smaller cucumbers were the ones that we got paid more money for; therefore, finding big cucumbers was bad.

Once the five-gallon bucket was full, we would have to carry it to the end of the row and dump the cucumbers into burlap sacks. It was not uncommon to get ten to twenty buckets off a pair of rows, or even more at times, depending on what time of the season we were in. We would break for lunch at midday. We would normally have peanut butter and jelly sandwiches, sardines, and crackers, sandwiches made of spam or little cans of potted meat. We would have Kool-Aid and water to drink. We keep gallons of water out in the fields to combat dehydration, but there was a bigger danger: rattlesnakes would often be in the cucumber fields, hiding under the leaves. I can safely say that it was by the grace of God that none of us were ever bitten by a snake; there were several close calls, but no one was ever bitten. Killing snakes was a common thing on the farm and especially in the fields. My dad never picked the cucumbers because he was busy working the farm for the rich white owners, but he warned us every day to be on the lookout for snakes. Strangely enough, he never told us what to do if we should get bitten by one, but it all worked out; we were never bitten, but we killed several rattlesnakes.

I can remember my brother Eugene visiting us and working in the field with us, and lo and behold, we ran across a ground rattler, a big one. Eugene killed this one and, to our surprise, said, "Don't you want to eat something other than peanut butter and jelly today?" Everyone in the field said no, except my stepbrother and me.

Eugene took his kill home, skinned it, floured it up like chicken, and waited for us to come home for lunch. When we got there, he began to fry it, and the pieces in the skillet began to move. To us kids, we were wondering if he had really killed the snake the right way, but he said that it was just the nerves in the snake and reminded us of how chickens continued to move after we cut their throats. (We grew our own chickens and butchered them as needed for food.) I don't remember what it tasted like, but when my father got home for lunch, we had already eaten, but he was really upset with Eugene for feeding us rattlesnake.

Eugene told my dad that one of the first things he did was cut the head off so that no one would be poisoned. My father then asked, "How do you know he didn't bite himself?" That questioned stumped Eugene, and the only reply he could come up with was "Well, I didn't think of that." We then began to try to vomit the snake up, but it was too late. Howard saved the day by telling us that the venom of a rattlesnake would have already taken effect if we were poisoned. That was good enough for me, and we went back to the cucumber field.

After we completed picking all the cucumbers for the day and putting them in sacks, the boys would be responsible for loading them up into the old black-and-white station wagon. We would lay the two rows of back seats down, crawl around, and get all of the sacks loaded up in the station wagon. Sometimes we would have to tie some of the sacks on top of the car. When my dad got off work, we would take them to the cucumber shed where all cucumbers were being bought. The white owners controlled this operation, as they did all things, and they got their cut regardless. When I became thirteen years old, my father tasked me with making sure that the station wagon was loaded and told me to drive the car to the cucumber shed as soon as we finished loading it up. He would then come later to help us. The cucumber shed was only about four miles from the field, and this was exciting at first, but later it became a lot of hard work and provided me no extra benefits.

After a few weeks, my father turned the responsibility over to me totally and seldom came to the cucumber shed. Howard had graduated, and the only other boys around were my stepbrother, Lee, and my half-brother, Leelin (first child of my father and stepmother). Leelin was pretty young, and it was hard to get Lee to follow through on anything. Most of the burden fell on my shoulders. Sanguretta would have helped, but my father would have none of that; he thought that there were too many boys around the cucumber shed. I told him that there were other girls there too, but that didn't matter to him.

He told me that I needed to start growing up and be a man and that he was not going to be around all the time. I was only thirteen—okay, closer to fourteen—but I was still just a kid. In the country, kids had huge responsibilities; I was driving at the age of thirteen, but only to places that involved working. By the age of fourteen, I knew how to operate the cornmeal presser, tractors, and bulldozers. I knew how to operate this machinery but was steered by my father to pay more attention to studying whenever I had the opportunity.

Well, I sucked it up and did as I was told. Big would push Lee to help constantly, but when we got to the cucumber shed, I had no authority to make him do anything. However, there would always be a few boys at the shed who would help me. After a few years of this, I toughened up and was capable of handling the task.

Memories of the Past

Edmund Pettus Bridge

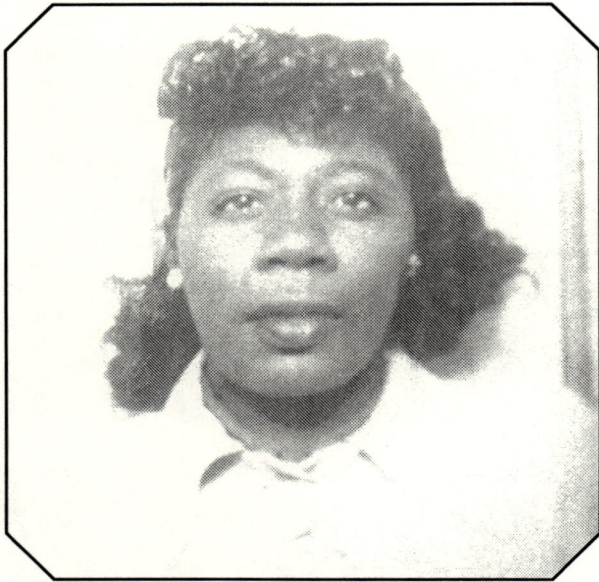

Patsy Lee Mosley Coker

Amy Lee Bell (Hun) 1981

Lee Earnest Coker - 1965

Family Picture - December 1959

Family Picture - 1965

Home - 1976

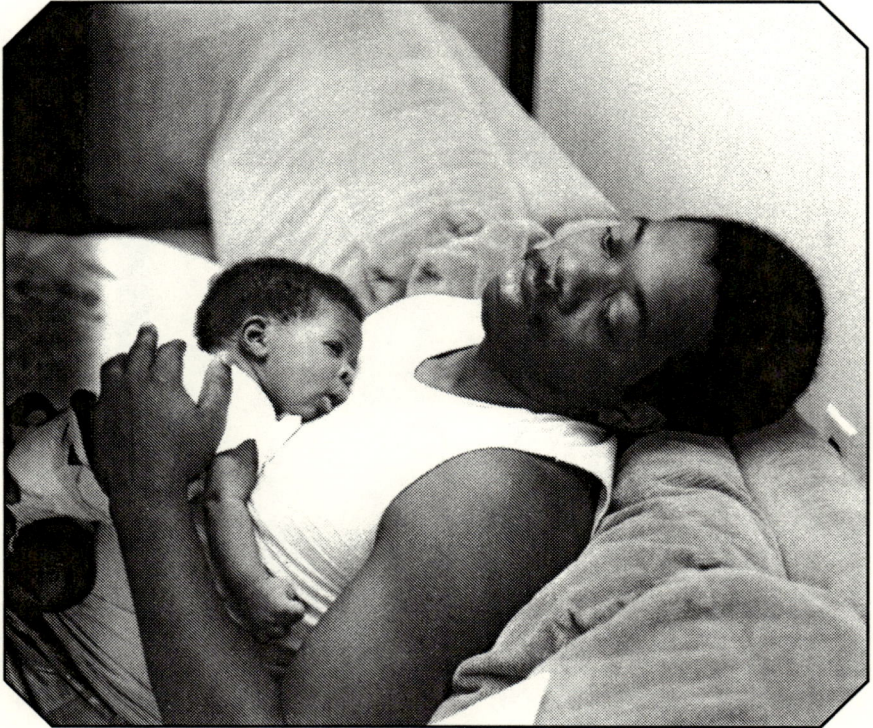

Nathan with Dad - December 1987

Ashley with Dad - 1993

Derrick with Dad - Summer 1997

Family Christmas 2006

Chapter 19 Summer in Pensacola

At the end of cucumber season, when I was fourteen years old, my father allowed me go and stay with my oldest brother, James, in Pensacola for the rest of the summer, which was about six weeks. My sister-in-law (Julia) assured my father that I could work with her cleaning up the movie theater where she worked; that was all he needed to hear, as long as I was busy. It was great being in Pensacola because it was the complete opposite of living in Sardis with my father.

For this period, I had running water and good kitchen appliances, and for the first time I could take a shower and step into the pleasure of feeling cold air during the summer from an air conditioner. As mentioned earlier, none of these luxuries were afforded by the Coker family in Sardis, Alabama. Being in Pensacola meant that for six weeks I had no chores—at least none to mention compared to being in Sardis on the farm.

The time in Pensacola allowed me to be exposed to fast food. Many of these restaurants were within walking distance of James and Julia's home. They were not rich, but compared to what I had been accustomed to, I was in heaven and truly appreciated the opportunity given me by James and Julia to live life differently, at least for a month. I am convinced that because of my time in Pensacola, I was able to live outside of the limited dimensions placed in my mind from life in Sardis, Alabama and expand my vision of dreams.

One of the most important differences was FREEDOM. This is easy to explain. There was none at my father's house, but in Pensacola I had more freedom than I had ever dreamed of in my life. I was expected to help keep the kitchen clean—that was it—and since they had running water, this was a breeze for me. I made deals with my nieces and nephew, Theodis, to do the dishes. In return, I would receive money, IOUs, and favors, all of which came in handy. Since I knew how to cook, I did this also to help and received a few dollars here and there for cooking. I have always liked cooking and would have done it for nothing, except money was given to me for doing it, so I took it. Other than these tasks, I was free to do what I wanted for the most part.

My brother lived in a neighborhood where everybody knew each other, so it was relatively safe as long as the people in the neighborhood didn't kill one another. Seriously, though, they all got along with each other for the most part. There were no strangers in the neighborhood, and when I arrived, within a day everyone knew that James's baby brother had come to visit.

My brother James had a reputation for being a great fisherman. He would go fishing at night and come back early in the morning with a cooler full of fish and sometimes a sack of shrimp. We would spend the early morning cleaning fish and shrimp and would normally have a fish fry the next day. Everyone in the neighborhood looked to James when it came to fishing; other men would stop by to check out his catch or share fishing information. He was like the weatherman of fishing and seemed to know the facts of every fishing spot within a twenty-five-mile radius of his home. James knew when the fish were biting, where they were, what fish were in each lake, and what bait to use at each of these lakes to get the fish biting. When he went fishing, it was safe to say that when he returned, we had a job for hours of cleaning fish and shrimp.

James and Julia loved to go to the racetrack and clubs, so I hung out with Theodis and his friends most of the time. (Theodis was the only boy that James and Julia had.) I was only two years older than Theodis, and we got along extremely well.

We would go out during the day riding bicycles all over the neighborhood and into Tate and Ensley. The other boys in the neighborhood accepted me, but they had their own form of initiation. I first had to prove myself to them. So I had to wrestle with each one of them to be accepted. Kenny was first, and I think he went easy on me because he was Theodis best friend. Shelia, who was Kenny's sister, said that we all were a bunch of idiots. But there were other girls watching, and for the second time in my life, I felt important through the observation of the opposite sex. I won the next three matches, and now the next opponent was Earl.

Earl and Kinney lived right behind Theodis, and I really felt bad about wrestling Kinney and now Earl, so I said that I'd had enough for one day. But Earl was very insistent. There was one thing that changed my mind. No, not the persistence of Earl, but the sweet smile and stare of Becky Ann Washington. She was like a thirteen-year-old version of Mary Jane Wilson; at least she had the same effect on me, and for some reason she had her eyes on me even though other boys, including Earl, had their eyes on her. At first, I thought that she was looking at someone else near me, beside me, or behind me, but Theodis said, "Somebody is looking at ya." I thought to myself, *What could she possible see in me?*

So Earl became my fifth wrestling opponent that day, and for once, I was glad that my father had fed and worked me the way he did. Earl was no competition; not only did he lose quickly, but he also sprained his wrist in the match. I looked to see where Becky Ann was, and to my surprise, she was talking to Theodis. Theodis called me to come over.

I was already beginning to think negatively, thinking that there was probably some joke on me coming up. Then he introduced her to me as his cousin, Becky Ann. So now my negative feeling changed to total disgust; I was thinking that this was family, so she must be off limits. So then I asked Theodis how was she related, and he said by a cousin of his mother, Julia. I then burst out and said, "That's all right, man!" They laughed at me and we walked Becky Ann home. Theodis was doing most of the talking while Becky Ann and I would try to look at each other without the other seeing it.

When we got in front of Becky Ann's house, I heard her father shouting at her to come inside. She grabbed my hand, said, "I'm glad that you are here," and ran inside. I looked at Theodis and said, "I ain't never going back to Alabama." It was only day two, and already I was fitting in with the boys of the neighborhood, had a couple of ways to make a little cash, and most of all, had the possibility of having a girlfriend who was pretty and had personality. These types of things just didn't happen to me; I had always bore the brunt of others' jokes or the harsh reality of them trying to take advantage of me or put me or my family down. For the first time in my life, I was experiencing this strange thing of being popular. I had found a fountain of popularity in this Pensacola community and was enjoying every minute of it.

That night all I could think about was Becky Ann Washington. This was just my second day in Pensacola, and if the rest of the summer was anything like this day, I knew leaving would be hard. When Julia got home, she told me that she wanted me to work with her and Theodis to clean up the theater and that we should sleep for a few hours and around 2:00 a.m. leave to go the theater. I asked here if she was joking, and then Theodis said, "Becky Ann will be there." Julia picked up on this like a dry sponge in water and said, "You only been here a day and you already have a girlfriend." I didn't know how to feel about any of this, but inside I felt like some victory had been won. I then replied to Julia that I would be glad to go and she said, "I bet you will."

A few minutes later, the phone rang and it was for Theodis. He talked a few minutes, laughing and clowning around, and then he said, "It's for you." It was Becky Ann; I was so shocked that I was speechless. (These types of things just didn't happen to me.) She then said, "Don't you have anything to say to me?" I regrouped and told her, "Yes, I hear that we will be working together in the theater tonight." She couldn't believe it and told me to stop joking. By now I was able to talk. I told her that this day was the best day of my life because I had met her. That statement shocked her a little bit and all she could say was that she would see you tonight.

I tried to sleep a few hours by listening to the radio, but it seemed as if every song played reminded me of Becky Ann, especially, "Tell Me Something Good" and "Rock the Boat." I eventually went to sleep and was shortly awaken by Julia saying that it was time to go to clean the theater. So we headed off and picked up Becky Ann, her older sister Esther, and her mother. Becky Ann and Esther were both racing to sit in the back seat because none of the kids wanted to sit between the two adults. Becky Ann lost this time and had to sit between the two women. We could tell in the back that she was ticked about the whole situation. Becky Ann's mother began a conversation with me, and within a few minutes, she asked me, "How do you like Pensacola?" I replied by saying that I was really enjoying myself and loved the atmosphere.

Esther then said, "That's not the only thing he loves." Then Becky Ann began to tell Esther to shut up. This seemed to make Esther tell even more. So now her mother knew that I had the hots for Becky Ann. Her mother then asked me, "What did my daughter do for you to love her?" I didn't know what to say, so I just told her the truth.

I told her that where I was from nobody really liked me and that we were extremely poor. I told her that kids and their parents made fun of us because we were taught to make something of ourselves. Esther interrupted me, saying, "What does that have to do with Becky Ann?" I then said, "Because Becky Ann is different. She accepted me and liked me the way that I am; she is pretty and has a sweet personality." For a minute, there was total silence, and then it was like a cloud full of laughter that burst. Everyone in the car was laughing; I mean laughing hard, except Becky Ann and me. By the time the laughing stopped, we were at the theater. As everyone was going inside, Becky Ann's mother told me that she thought I was a special young man and that I shouldn't do anything to change that opinion, but she told me that her husband was not understanding and that he was not in favor of Becky Ann seeing any boy. I asked, "So I can't see Becky Ann anymore?" She said, "No, I am not saying that. Becky Ann knows her father and how to stay out of trouble."

We broke up into two teams; Becky Ann and I were on separate teams. Each team had to clean half of the theater. So after a few hours of work, it was time to take a break. Finally Becky Ann and I were able to talk for a few minutes. She was really moved by how I felt about her and told me that no one had ever said these nice things about her, and unexpectedly, she kissed me. I hadn't been kissed since the day Mary Jane Wilson kissed me in the closet. (Aunts and family members don't count.) We kissed again for just a little while longer, and then Theodis interrupted and began to laugh. We then took off running after him.

When we caught him, he said that he was going to tell if we didn't help him get into the candy stand at the theater. I was opposed to stealing, but I wanted to see Becky Ann again and the theater was a good way to see her. So Becky Ann and I agreed to help him on one condition and that being that he just keep his cousin Esther occupied so that she would not be snooping around Becky Ann and me. We tried but ran out of time on our break, so we put it off to the next night and had success.

As far as my relationship with Becky Ann was concerned, we were tight most of the summer; not a day went by that we didn't spend hours together. Sometimes it was going to the store, working in the theater, going to church, and walking the neighborhood, babysitting, or just hanging out around Theodis house. Becky Ann would also come over to the basketball games in the neighborhood to watch me play. While in Pensacola, I played better than ever and I built a reputation for being a great player and would always be among the first to get picked. I couldn't explain it, it seemed as if everything I touched in Pensacola was turning to gold. When I played sports (especially basketball), I was extremely good. I was hitting the majority of the points on whatever team I played on, and my defense was quick and aggressive. No matter where I took the shot from, it went in. Between games, I would share a soda and a kiss or two with Becky Ann and go play some more. After many of the games, other kids would ask what team I played on back home and if my team went to the state championships. I would tell them the truth: that I didn't play on any team and probably wasn't good enough. They laughed at me and said that many of them were starters in their school and that I could start if I came to their school. Many of them thought that I should be in a summer league.

Hearing these things helped me tremendously and reminded me of all the days and nights that I shot basketball alone several hours in the dark and how I so desperately wanted to play but could not because of my father. Each scenario came true of having to make three, four, five, or even six shots in a row and having no fear to take the shot, but it was playing defense too. I wasn't very tall, but I noticed that tall players were not as fast as me, and they did not handle the ball as well either. Their comments brought me happiness, but a little sadness also because I knew that I would never play on my school's team and that the summer had to come to an end.

As Becky Ann would stare into my eyes up close to me and ask, "What's the matter?" I would take her by the hand and would tell her why I would never play any sport in school. Her reply was that this was terrible and that if I kept playing like I did while there in Pensacola, I would be a star on some team. I grabbed her and said, "I play like this only because of you." She would tell me that I was just full of it and we would move on to the next thing.

I should have known that things were too good to last. Disaster struck at the end of my fourth week in Pensacola. There was a block party in the neighborhood on the same street that my brother lived on. Theodis and I were there early, and Becky Ann was coming later with other girls on her block. A girl from the neighborhood, Madeline, came up to me and started talking to me. She must have been talking to someone about me because she knew where I was from and how much longer I would be staying. She then said that she had seen me play basketball and was impressed and would like me to teach her how to play. So her younger brother threw a basketball to me and I began to show her simple dribbling techniques. She then began to guard me, and when I turned my back to make a move with the ball, she grabbed me and kissed me.

Next thing I remember was hearing Becky Ann call my name, and it wasn't a good call. She came up to me, struck me in the mouth, and was ready to fight Madeline. A few more fellows got in the middle to break it up. Theodis and my nieces were there and for a minute were shocked due to what they had seen. One of my nieces began to talk to Becky Ann and tell her that it didn't happen the way that she was thinking. In the meantime, my lip was bleeding and I was looking for some ice to put on it. I began to see now that this love thing could hurt; I also saw that Becky Ann was a bit jealous and could be mean at times. We kids went home after that.

Well, later that night, Becky Ann called me and said that she was sorry, that she trusted me, and that she wanted to see me. We devised a plan; I would walk to the corner nearest to her house, and when I got to the corner, whistle. So I got to the corner of her house and tried to whistle, but because my lip was swollen, I had great difficulty, but she heard me anyway. She came out and apologized again, kissed me, and said, "Don't you ever kiss another girl again but me." I kissed her again and said, "I will see you tomorrow." When my brother got home, he asked me who had hit me in the mouth. One of my nieces told him the whole story; he found the whole thing extremely funny. When he finally stopped laughing, he told me that I had better be careful or women trouble could make me drink; he started back to laughing at me again.

That wasn't the end of my trouble. Theodis and I were outside most of the time. One day I noticed that there was someone peeping out of the window of the house next door, so I asked Theodis about it. He told me that her name was Rosaline and that her family was very religious and did not want their children to talk or associate with other kids in the neighborhood. The next day, I saw Rosaline going to catch the bus to go to camp. I offered to walk her to the bus stop, and she said okay. As we were talking, I felt sorry for her because I knew what it was like to be in a house with rigid, restricting, and controlling parents.

Later on that night, Rosaline met me at the fence, and we began to talk about things. She asked if I had a girlfriend, and I told her about Becky Ann. She said that she couldn't see why I would want to be with Becky Ann. Her parents got home and she had to go before they knew she was talking to me, and that was the end of our conversation for that night.

When I went inside, Becky Ann had just called me. She was really mad at me and told me that if I wanted Rosaline I could have her but that she never wanted to see me again. How could she have known that fast? Someone had to be watching to report it to her that soon. That night Becky Ann didn't come to the theater and Esther was glad to tell me that Becky Ann didn't want to see me again. I was so upset that I spoke to Julia, my sister-in-law, about it; she told me that Becky Ann would probably cool off in a few days. So I called her the next day, but she would not talk to me. I called the next day—still nothing. Then Theodis told me that Monroe was bragging about Becky Ann kissing him. Theodis called Becky Ann to see what was going on. She told him that she was moving on with Earl, but Theodis said that she wanted to get back at me for kissing Rosaline. I then replied that that never happened. Theodis replied that it was Monroe who told Becky Ann all of this. Theodis told Monroe that I was going to get him for doing that and that he had violated the "guy trust" thing by telling. That same day, we saw Becky

Ann and Monroe walking past the house. I called Monroe and told him that I wanted to talk to him with Theodis beside me, but Monroe began to run and ran home. So Becky Ann got mad at me again and we had a big argument right there in the street. Later that night, Monroe apologized and said that he would not be a part of Becky Ann's plan, but I told him that it didn't matter because I was moving on with Rosaline. Some of this was feelings for Rosaline, but some was to get back at Becky Ann.

I decided that since I was already condemned, I might as well go on and talk to Rosaline. So that night, Rosaline and I started meeting at the fence each night and I would walk her to the bus stop for the next couple of weeks. During this whole time, there was no communication between Becky Ann and me, but I thought of her every day. She would call the house and talk to Theodis, but she would not even ask to speak to me. Theodis would always say, "You better go on and make up with your girlfriend," and I would reply that things were okay with Rosaline. He would pop me in the head, saying, "You know who I am talking about."

Two days before I had to leave to go back to Sardis, Alabama, Becky Ann came over to my brother's house with some friends and was doing a good job of ignoring me, but when I saw her again, I knew that I could not leave Pensacola this way; she had done a lot to help my self-confidence. I didn't care what anyone else thought—she was special to me, and I just could not let things end this way between us.

I went to her in front of her friends and asked her if we could talk. She said, "What do you want to say to me? You can say it in front of my friends." I took her hand and told her that my life would never be the same because of her and that I did not want to leave knowing that things were not right between us and that I wished we could be together again. I told her that I would always love her, no matter what happened between us. She then said, "Why did you tell me this in front of everybody?" and she hugged me really tight. We then took a private walk around the block, talking and holding hands. Becky Ann told me that I had to leave Rosaline alone and I said I would. I didn't have to; Rosaline saw me walking with Becky Ann and refused to talk to me again. But I didn't care because no one had affected me like Becky Ann.

On my last night in Pensacola, one of the kids in the neighborhood was having a birthday party and we all went. Becky Ann and I only danced with each other and spent all the other time together that night. Well, 10:30 p.m. came before we knew it, and it was time to go home. Theodis and I walked Becky Ann and Esther home. On the way to Becky's home, we stopped many times to embrace and share a kiss and one final time in front of her house, and then I heard her father's voice saying "Come on inside."

So my last day with Becky Ann ended, just like my first day had begun, me thinking about her all night. There were no cell phones, so we could not carry on our conversation. We both made a promise to see each other the next summer. It was really hard leaving, but a man's got to do what a man's got to do.

The next summer, with a little more than six weeks, I returned to Pensacola with a great heart to see Becky Ann. Basketball and wrestling was about the same, but Becky Ann had a boyfriend. We still saw each other and not long afterward, she broke up with him; at least that's what she told me. Things had changed, and it was apparent that she didn't feel the same about me as she had that first summer. I guess you could say that 50 percent of the time that I was there we were a couple, but it had transitioned into a love/hate relationship. So I had no other choice but to see other girls. I tried talking to Rosaline again, but that didn't work.

Playing basketball took Theodis and me into Lincoln, Ensley, and Tate, where I met Betty. Betty's brother was on the team for Tate High School, so my neighborhood team played against his team. Many people began to stop and watch because he was good and his team played well together. I had continued to play, shooting at the goal on the back of the old pecan tree in the back of the yard on the farm, still shooting at night when I could get away with it. I had gotten to the point that if I made a few shots in a row, I could make shots without concentrating on the basket.

With many spectators watching, they took an early lead, but we fought back and I was able to get into a good rhythm and would just catch and shoot. We tied the score, and the game went into deuce. They threw the ball in, but I was able to make a steal, turn around, and shoot for the lead. They tied it up again, and this went on and on until it started to get dark; they wanted to quit, but I demanded that we finish it. Therefore, we keep playing. With the game tied up, I got the ball, their whole team came towards me, and I bounced the ball from the corner to the center, thinking that someone had to be open. Sure enough, one of my teammates took it in for an uncontested lay-up. They missed their next shot, and my center threw it out to me for a long shot. I took the shot and, as everyone was looking, we could all hear the ball rattle in the basket. We had won this long game of a few hours.

By now, it was too late to talk to Betty, so I promised her that I would call her that night and said that we had to get home before any of the adults. Betty's brother asked us to come back and play when we could; this became a regular event for Theodis and me, but we decided to cut the future games short so that we could socialize the girls. (For me, it was just Betty.)

Chapter 20 We Stick Together

Living on the farm always allowed us to eat fresh food, but at the time, we didn't see the blessing in this; we considered it as a negative side effect of being poor. We had cornbread every day with greens (collards, cabbage, turnip, or mustard) or neck bones and rice or butter beans or black-eyed peas. We often made our own cornmeal until the mill generator broke and it wasn't profitable for the sharecropper owners.

On one occasion, we had black-eyed peas two or three times within the last week and we were having them again. All of us sat down, prayed, and began to eat our cornbread, fatback, and black-eyed peas—all of us except for Sanguretta. Sanguretta said what all we kids were thinking about: "Um tired of peas; I don't want no more peas." As she said this, we all were stricken with fear of what my father was going to do. He surprised us by not whipping Sanguretta. Instead, he told her to get up from the table and not eat anything. She had to go to bed without eating anything.

Later on that night, after everyone had gone to bed, Sanguretta and Rebecca (our stepsister) got up. Their goal was to sneak into the kitchen and eat some of the leftovers without anyone knowing about it. I heard them getting up but pretended to be asleep. They made it into the kitchen, and Rebecca lifted the top of the pot to the peas and Sanguretta was poised to scoop out a healthy portion. Right at that time, the lights came on; it was my father turning on the light and saying, "Go on to bed NOW and leave that pot alone 'fore I git a limb for you." She was very close to it but lost it all at the pull of a string of the light in the kitchen by our father. I don't remember Sanguretta ever complaining about food on the table again. The very next day, we had peas again.

It is hard to believe that we didn't kill ourselves growing up because some of the things we did were extremely dangerous. One spring break, when we were out of school for a week, in the middle of the week, Sanguretta and I began to have an argument over something. Sanguretta was a great debater, so there was no way that I was going to win the argument. Knowing this from experience, I decided to throw something up that would change the focus of the conversation. She had a boyfriend; let's call him JR. We teased her all the time about him, calling him every kind of name you could think of that parents would not want to hear they children say, such as "lurch, fish-eyed, bug-faced, monster breath, etc."

Okay, I know that those names are nothing nowadays compared to what you hear kids say, but then they were something. He deserved those names and worse because he was only after one thing from as many girls as he could get. This my father and I agreed on, and we made a pack. My dad told me to keep an eye on JR and keep him informed. I had no problem with this because JR never had any respect for my family. Often he would mock my dad and make jokes about Howard, my brother, and make fun of how poor the Coker family was in Selma. It was okay for us to badmouth each other, but this was not a privilege for those who had no Coker blood running in their veins.

Therefore, I began to rag on JR, repeating things that he had said about different family members. This got other family members involved and cast them into the conversation, hurling insults at JR and his family. I stepped up the attack by saying every kind of personal insult that I could think of. I could tell that I had Sanguretta close to the boiling point. Within a few minutes, she grabbed the butcher knife and began chasing me through the house.

I ran out the door and around the house, but just could not shake her. I then ran back in the house, slamming doors behind me to slow her up; but this only increased her anger. In the background, I could hear the rest of the family telling her to stop chasing me with the knife, but it fell on deaf ears. She was really mad and wanted to do bodily damage to me. I ran back into the kitchen, where it all started, and was running out of places to go, so I ran straight into the kitchen screen door. The force was so great that when I ran into the screen door, it flew off the hinges and went about ten feet from the house. I was floating on the screen door for about ten feet before it hit the ground in a muddy spot.

After this happened; it was like we were all frozen in time like something you would see on "Star Trek" or the "Matrix". Everyone in the house had forgotten what the dispute was about and was totally focused on the new problem at hand. This seemed to cause Sanguretta to snap out of her rage of anger. Everyone in the house, including my grandfather Ike (this was before he passed away), became extremely worried because we all knew that when my father got home, there was going to be hell to pay. So we all worked to put things back in place. We knew that we would not be able to avoid punishment by my father, but we just wanted to limit the damage that was due to come. A couple of my older brothers realigned the hinges in the wall. Sanguretta and I cleaned the mud off the screen and tried to smooth out the screen-door imprint that was in the mud on the side of the house. Together, we got the screen door back on the hinges. It was amazing. What had started as an argument and had led to a threat on my life ended up as a family project.

When my dad got home, we all waited to see how long it would take him to recognize what had happened. It was about an hour before he began to fuss at us. He didn't whip us this time, but said some very hurtful things to Sanguretta and me. I don't remember what he said, but I do remember that he yelled at us for more than an hour; I would have much preferred to get a whipping than hear all that verbal abuse.

We never picked on any other kids in school, but other children always made fun of us. Many of them made fun of how poor we were, our outhouse, and the clothes that we wore. They joked about my father's lack of education and how he spoke (even though their own parents were no better off than our father was). They talked about us because we were committed to school and doing the best we could do. They criticized us because my father would not let us hang out with them; instead, we had to do chores, work, and do school work.

Back during those times, boys in the senior class were given jobs to drive the school buses. Our bus driver was notorious for making fun of my family, and Sanguretta and I had little tolerance for being subjects of such humor. One day the bus driver went too far and began belittling my brother, Howard. He called him weak, hopeless, and many other unpleasant names, which I will not mention. This was on top of already downing my father and family. We might have been bad off and yes our father was a character, but we were a family and he was our dad, the one given us by the Father and we were taught not to let anyone put us down.

I could not take any more, and when he stopped the bus at the next stop, I took my lunch bucket (an old metal-looking maple syrup bucket that we had made into a lunch bucket) and swung it in the direction of the young man driving the bus. Right away he began bleeding from a big gash on his forehead. He then stopped the bus and grabbed me, and that's when Sanguretta lit into him also. At that point, we all flew out of the bus. My cousins got involved also. I think some other black parents happened to notice and came over and broke it up. The bus driver was bloody, and we had blood all over us also, but it wasn't our blood, and that was what counted. The bus driver got back on the bus and refused to let Sanguretta, my cousins, and me back on the bus.

When my father got home from work, he already knew about it. I often wonder how he got so much information during those days when he worked out in isolated fields and swamps. Keep in mind that there was no phone of any kind during those days in our neighborhood. This is one time that I remember my father giving us a break. He yelled at us, threatened to beat us, and told us that we must learn to ignore such insults. He also told us that we did the right thing to stand up for the family but that we should try to do it more peacefully the next time.

He took us to school the next day and spoke with the principal. We confessed to what we did and what had happened. We were excused and sent to class. Later on that day, we were told that it was okay for us to ride the bus but that I could not sit on the seat that was right behind the bus driver. When we got on the bus, the driver said not a word to us or about us, or anyone else for that matter. He had a big bandage on his forehead, and even though other kids were trying to get things started again, he remained quiet and so did we.

Chapter 21 Hit by Integration

*I*n 1973, we were faced with integration in the South; prior to this time, all the black children in Sardis attended Shiloh High School. We didn't have the luxuries there of the white schools, but we had a sense of community and belonging; it was our school and we took care of it. The teachers and the principal had total control. I remember having devotion each morning before classes would start. We would sing a song, say the Pledge of Allegiance, and have a prayer. It brought us closer together, and we kids looked forward to it.

February was very special because it was deemed Black History Month, and we would sing "We Shall Overcome" and the black man's national anthem, "Lift Every Voice and Sing." Integration would bring all these special events to an end. Don't get me wrong; during that time in the South, it had to be so, even if it meant not being able to keep some cultural traditions. After all, culture identification must occur within the heart and mind first before becoming an icon of tradition, and once there, there is nothing that can replace it.

Shiloh High School became Shiloh Jr. High. Howard had graduated and was attending the University of Arizona. My sister Sanguretta was the first to go to Southside High School, which had previously been an all-white school in rural Selma. The atmosphere was thick with hate and racism. One of Sanguretta's classes in particular was very difficult. The teacher was Mrs. Hardison (a member of a very racist white family). She had all the black kids answer "yes, ma'am" and "no, ma'am," while the white kids could simple say yes or no.

One day Sanguretta responded by saying yes. Mrs. Hardison became irate and got in my sister's face, and then I believe the weight of racism on Sanguretta surfaced to the point that an equal if not equivalent reaction needed to be released. As Mrs. Hardison attempted to put her hands on Sanguretta, Sanguretta pushed her away and ready to attack her, but some of the other black kids held her back. When the story got to the principal's office, Mrs. Hardison lied, saying that my sister had attacked her. In the office, they didn't even listen to the story from the black kids, but when the white kids began to tell the story, it made a difference. They all swore that Mrs. Hardison always treated the black kids differently; that she treated them like secondary citizens. They told the principal that Mrs. Hardison made all the black kids say "yes, ma'am" and "no, ma'am" to her and that it was Mrs. Hardison who approached my sister.

I told Sanguretta that she should have let my father come, but she didn't want him to come to the school and get excited. It was certain that he would have made a major scene and embarrassed the family. During this tribulation, many students, black and white, gave their support to Sanguretta, and some of the teachers did so as well. There were a couple of teachers who had been transferred from Shiloh Jr. High who led the support for my sister.

There was no suspension, but Sanguretta did have to write a letter of apology for touching Mrs. Hardison. Mrs. Hardison from that time on never required the black kids to respond with "yes, ma'am" and "no, ma'am." This didn't change the South, but it did much for our existence in Sardis because talk of Sanguretta's actions went around to other schools. In a society where victory for the black people was rare, it was good to see the courage of my sister encourage others to stand up for their rights and beliefs.

It has not been many years since we witnessed the Jim Crow laws of Selma and how some of the white policemen released the dogs and water hoses on our people. As a little boy, I will never forget what happened in Selma that day; it is an image that has been locked in my mind and that I cannot free myself from. So when Sanguretta stood firm on being equal and won some recognition, we thought of the event of the prejudiced South that led up to that moment with Mrs. Hardison.

Because of integration, many changes were occurring in the South. In Sardis, Alabama, Shiloh High School had become first grade through ninth grade, and students from Minter, Alabama, were being bused to Shiloh (a little more than an hour on the bus). Even though Shiloh was integrated, there were no white students sent there, but many of the black teachers of Shiloh were sent to white schools and many white teachers were sent to Shiloh. This started in my eighth-grade year. I remember the great teacher, Mr. Chapman, my music teacher. Don't misunderstand; I was only in that class because my father insisted. Somehow someone had put it in his head that music would make us better people. I didn't share his thought and had a great desire to play football. This year was the first year that Shiloh Jr. High would be having a middle-school football team.

I was the ultimate sportsman. I would watch sporting event as much as I could. It didn't matter what the sport was; I was interested. Likewise, I wanted to play, but because of father, I was not able to play any sports on any of the teams. It was the same story from my father, "You will get hurt. Who is going to pay for doctor visits or hospital? I'm sending you to school to get an education, not to get broken up. I expect you to have all As in school." The fact that football practice was at the same time as the music class did not help my case any either.

The football coach, Mr. Leeman, had watched me from sixth and early seventh grade in PE and thought that I had some natural ability to play quarterback and pretty good speed. Well, I was all for it, but my father wasn't. I hated music but was forced to do it by my father. So while I was in the music class, I looked out the window only to see others practicing and enjoying the pleasure that I would only dream about. There I was in music, at least physically, but my spirit was out on the football practice field. You wouldn't believe how I daydreamed about playing football, making the big play, being surrounded by the girls, and yes, having a favorite girl that I could call my girlfriend—and *BAM*! Not BAMA, but *BAM*! That would be the sound of Mr. Chapman slamming a book on my desk to get my attention. Well, after the first week, he thought it would be wise to move me from the front near the windows, but found out that I still daydreamed and fantasized about touching the old pig skin, enjoying the thrill of running into others, and having them hitting and meeting as human mobile missiles seeking a target. Not even the threat, the agony, or the terror brought on from my father could shake my desire to play.

Somehow, I managed to get an A out of that class. I don't know how, but I just remember that when the final grade was given, I had an A for my grade. Mr. Chapman told me that he knew how bad I wanted to play and he wished that he could have helped me, but it was out of his hands. He also said that even though my heart was somewhere else, he was impressed at my attention to complete the work in his class.

Shiloh was more than just a school. During that time, we prayed and recited the Pledge of Allegiance every day before classes would start; at this time, the ACLU was busy fighting causes for those who needed help protecting their rights. We had a village where most of the teachers cared about the students and their people. Don't get me wrong; there were some bad teachers, but there were some that were great leaders in some way or another, and if there was or is a hall of fame for teachers, then they should have a spot.

Who could forget Mrs. Vatelle, the librarian, who taught not only how to do research in the library and library etiquette but etiquette that would last a lifetime. I now look back and thank her for challenging me to read for fun and to never stop learning—to read all kinds of books about all kinds of things. One of her thoughts was that you should not be afraid to learn something, but more important, she emphasized the need for a black man to get an education.

This would be strongly supported by Mrs. Gertrude Pottison, who taught English, history, and social studies. I can remember Mrs. Pottison quoting Shakespeare to us wherever she saw us—even in front of my dad. He didn't understand it but supported it because Mrs. Pottison was a great supporter of education for all the kids at Shiloh.

She had taught some of my sisters and brothers before me and for years pushed them as well as me to push beyond our known limits to be better. She would always say, "There is nothing out of your reach, if you put your mind to it and commit to it. Mr. Coker, you could be president someday, if you have the desire." She would always say, "You are a Coker, marked for excellence; so go for it." This helped us to stay focused and not sell ourselves short to the stereotypes that were present and predetermined by a racist South. You see, there were plenty of white folks calling us niggers, putting us down, and disrespecting our parents and us. There were even some black folks who thought that we should never strive to have what the white man had. But through God, my father, and good teachers, we learned that it wasn't striving to have what the white man had, but instead it was striving to get what God has provided, what he has made available. It was and is called making use of opportunities. This applies even today because it is very important to not waste opportunities of blessings.

Chapter 22 Dealing with a Bully

*I*t wasn't always great experiences. One day while we were waiting for the bus after school, one of the school bullies, Willie Hill, choose to pick on Leelin, my half brother from my father side. Two teachers (Mrs. Pitts and Mrs. Helle) watched the whole thing but did nothing to make Willie stop. Willie and I both were in the eighth grade, but he was twice my size (maybe three times). I knew that I was no match for him, but I could not let him just push a family member around like that. Leelin was a few years younger, but that didn't matter; he was a Coker, and we stood together. So I asked Willie to leave him alone, knowing this would put me in jeopardy. Willie then began to push and attack me. I fought back, but I was no match for him. He was able to get his arms around me and picked me up and threw me in a puddle of muddy water. Then I heard Mrs. Helle and Mrs. Pitts running over and yelling at me for picking on Willie. Other friends said that I was very lucky because my head missed hitting a large rock in the puddle. So there were many laughing at me: Willie Hill, Mrs. Helle and Mrs. Pitts, and other students. I was surprised at Mrs. Helle and Mrs. Pitts and wondered why they had lied about what happened. Why and how did I become the bad guy, when I was only doing what they should have done? Well, for them and to them, I cursed the ground that they walked on, and from that point on, they became dead to me, but not to my father.

As I got on to the bus, wet and muddy, I can remember the kind words of Angie Mims, who had earlier found me a towel from somewhere. Angie was one of my best friends. So she sat beside me as many avoided me and asked, "What do you think your father is going to do?" I looked at Angie with a puzzled look as if to say, "Thanks for elevating this problem to a whole new level." I was so upset and embarrassed that I really hadn't given much thought to it. Angie then said, "I think your dad is coming to the school tomorrow."

Today my kids cringe when they think that I am coming to the school to discuss issues about them, but they have no idea of what it would be like if their school were visited by their grandfather, Lee Earnest Coker.

When my father got off work, he already knew; I think Leelin might have told him. I could hear him calling me as he approached the house. Normally, if we got beaten in a fight, my dad would whip us again for losing, but in this case, he remembered Willie because while he had visited the school for some other matter, he had made Willie stop picking on some other smaller kids. So he asked me what had happened. I told him the whole thing and Leelin told him how it started. My father got very angry and said, "I heard that your head nearly hit a big rock; do you know that you could have died? You know that I don't like to see people pushing you around like this, but Pop, I am glad that you stood up for your brother, even though the result turned out bad for you. You should always stand up for others. I'll take care of this."

The night passed, and the next morning I was wondering what my dad meant by saying "I'll take care of it." As we were getting ready for school, my dad told me that he was going to take me to school in the car. We were moving towards the car and my dad hesitated, starring at his guns (I was praying, oh Lord, please don't let him bring the guns). The prayer must have worked; my dad was interrupted by my stepmother for something and he began to argue a few minutes with her and lost sight of the guns.

So as we were driving to the school, my dad was talking about how sick he was of people bullying others around. It didn't take me long to reason that he was not just talking about Willie Hill, but also about being bullied around by the white dominance in the South, specifically in Sardis and Selma, Alabama.

When we got to the school, I saw Willie Hill getting off the bus; I was just hoping that my dad didn't see him. Oh, but he did. Never mind parking in a parking space. My dad drove the car sideways right up to the curb where Willie Hill was walking. He stopped and my dad jumped out of the car and told him, "Didn't I tell you to stop picking on other people's children a while back?" Willie responded with a timid "yah-sir." Then my dad said, "Well, why are you picking on my boys?" Now, everybody probably had heard some story of how my father got upset and maybe fired shots at various people. I believe that at that point, Willie probably thought about some of those crazy stories that he might have heard about my dad. I had never seen him so afraid. He began to tell my dad that he didn't mean anything by it. My father then told him that if he ever heard of him bothering a Coker again, that he (my father) would do no talking. We all understood what that meant. By this time, the principal came out and told my dad not to talk to the students about events that might have happened, but that he should talk to him, the principal. By now there were many students and some teachers gathered around watching. My father then told the principal, "If you had been doing your job, then I wouldn't be here right now. I got to miss work to come out here to do what you ought to be doing. I heard that you ridiculed Pop [oh, how I hated it when he used my nickname in public] for standing up for his little brother while you laughed it off with this troublemaker. Now, I don't want no trouble, but you didn't do right and I ain't gonna let you treat my children any kind of way." The principal then changed his tone and asked my father and me to come to the office. So my dad moved the car off the walkway, and I could see the veins in my father's neck and frowns in his forehead rising, indicating to me that things were going to get worse.

So we went to the office, my dad and I, with the principal. The principal asked me to tell them what had happened, so I did so. He then said that other students had told a similar story and that he was aware of issues with Willie Hill. My dad then told him that he (the principal) was to blame as well and that they had better do something because, if any of his kids got hurt, he would be back, and not to talk. So the principal said that he would take care of it and asked my dad if there was anything else, and my dad said, "Yeah, I want to talk to Mrs. Helle and Mrs. Pitts."

So I was told to wait outside the principal's office while Mrs. Helle and Pitts came to the office. They didn't know my father was in the office, and one of them said something else to me like, "Bet you will stop getting in the face of people bigger than you now!" I'm not sure what my father said, but there was some cursing and bits and pieces of dialog where my father told them that they were worthless old hags and bitter for no reason. The principal asked me to go to class, but I waited to see what would happen next. I could hear Mrs. Helle and Pitts try to manipulate the truth and talk down to my dad, but the principal was interjecting the comments of others and my dad was being himself. He, my dad, could put up with a liar much quicker than someone who tried to talk down to him. He tolerated it from white folk, but there was no way he would let other black people do it to him. He was ticked off with them and they were going to hurt before he left.

So toward the end of the discussion, I heard "Don't make me come back here looking for each one of you." Everyone else in the office heard that, and they all knew that he meant it.

When it was over, Mrs. Helle and Mrs. Pitts were in tears, the principal seemed exhausted, but my dad—not him; he had total joy on his face and in his heart and was ready to go to work and have a good day.

Chapter 23 The Other Side of Integration

---

*T*hen, there were the territorial disputes of kids from schools in Minter combining with those already at Shiloh. For those of us that were already going to Shiloh Jr. High, we thought that we had sovereignty rights. There were many fights at first, but we were constantly reminded of who the enemy was by their actions, and we soon discovered that we were not each other's enemy. Now, that didn't mean that there were no fights but that they just were not territorial battles. Fights during that time were nothing like fights in schools today. There were no guns, knives, or gangs. Things were always resolved without serious injury.

There were occasions when the girls would fight. Let me tell you; don't believe everything you see on TV. There was nothing sexual when these girls would fight, and many times their fights were worse than the boys' and seemed to be more vicious. The girls didn't just fight the girls but the boys as well. I can remember several occasions when girls would attack the boys. You might think that this was just a terrible thing for the boys to engage in, but from what I remember, at the end of each fight that was between a boy and a girl, the girl came out on top.

I remember on a spring day one of the boys said something very cruel and obnoxious about the mother and boyfriend of one of the girls. The boy was Earnest Jones and the girl was Patricia Goodman. The teacher started class as usual, and from the back of the class, we heard this loud slap.

Next there was the sound of chairs flying by, and they were not being thrown by Earnest but by Patricia. The teacher was Miss Tillman, a young white graduate who was not accustomed to this type of behavior. She immediately ran to the office. The rest of the boys in the class tried to break them up. Patricia's clothes were half torn off. (She was in her bra to some degree and her pants were ripped.) But it was worse for Earnest; he was bleeding and his shirt was ripped open. He had been kicked several times below the belt and hit by a flying chair, and his face looked like it had been hit with brass knuckles. As we were trying to stop them, we received collateral damage wounds and let them go back at it. Then we saw Earnest going through the window at the hands of Patricia, with broken glass going everywhere.

By this time, the principal and other teachers arrived and regained control. The class spent the next hour cleaning up the mess. Patricia and Earnest disappeared for the rest of the day and were both suspended for a few days. Everybody talked about that fight for weeks. I only remember one time when there was a fight between a boy and a girl, and it was questionable whether the girl held her own. In that fight, she slipped in heels, which caused the boy to get an advantage, which was stopped immediately. Fighting wasn't something that happened all the time, but when it happened, it was always a sight to remember.

Chapter 24 Discrimination by My Own People

One ideal that is expressed throughout the South is that white is better. For years, through slavery, this was the thought. Through emancipation, this was the thought. And through the years of Jim Crow laws, free reign of the Klan, and other white supremacists, known and unknown, this remained to be the prevailing thought, so much so that a large number of blacks even believed that white was better. I am not just talking about shoe polish but an idea that being white was better than being black any day.

Whites were not the only ones preoccupied by the color of your skin, but a large number of blacks were also. With many whites, 1 percent of black blood in one's veins made a person black even if 99 percent of their blood was made up of white genes, and they were unworthy to be a part of white society. Within the black society of the South, there existed a common form of discrimination. Not all but many blacks were a part of this unfair practice.

Blacks with a lighter skin complexion were given favoritism, or stating it another way, darker-skinned blacks were treated inferior to those of lighter complexion by many blacks in the South. This was not the doing of white people but of other black people who had bought into the idea that "white is better." These same blacks would shout at an MLK rally and "amen" the sermon to death but greatly lacked any depth of understanding of the dream of MLK—that no one "be judged by the color of their skin, but rather the content of their character."

My first encounter of this was in the first grade in Mrs. Wrong's class. It was addressed earlier in this book, but to refresh your memory, Mary Jane and I were in the closet and I was receiving my first kiss. When Mrs. Wrong opened the door, I received the harsh punishment of being dragged out of the supply closet, whipped with a yardstick, and hearing the teacher ridicule me verbally. Mary Jane, on the other hand, received no punishment. I believe to this day that this was because Mary Jane was very light-skinned.

School clubs were not exempt from this principle. When I was in elementary school, I remember the unfair practices of the clubs at Shiloh. The power and control of these clubs was in the hands of the elite, the chosen—those with lighter skin tones. The other less fortunate ones had to take what they gave or whatever was left over. It was like the white South was still controlling us on a micro level through the presence of our own people.

Other kids of lighter complexion could do no wrong. On many occasions, their lies were considered as gospel and their schoolwork was considered excellent, while others—including my sisters, brothers, myself, and other dark-skinned kids—were given a back seat. Not only did we have to overcome discrimination from whites, but we were also faced with the same problem from many blacks who could really affect our future.

When competing against them—the lighter-skinned blacks—we had to be better, and often we were, but we could not overcome the prejudiced judges. As a result, I learned that the best guy doesn't win all the time and that prejudices are not just between races, but can be within a race of people. You might ask then, why compete? The answer is because we learned to compete against ourselves in hopes that one day we would be on a fair playing field.

But it didn't happen at Shiloh High or Shiloh Jr. High. I can remember many teachers who practiced this prejudiced ideology against many of us kids. On a few occasions, I can remember a couple of these teacher telling me that no matter how good I was or did in school, they would not give me an A in their classes. Do you have any idea what this can do to a child? Even with my father fighting the battle, we could not beat inside prejudices of our people, but my father made us think in terms of tomorrow and gave us an attitude to keep on fighting and working to be the best at what we do.

There were many who were damaged beyond repair and could not overcome the racism and prejudices from their own people. Others didn't and don't like talking about this matter, but it was a reality and another challenge that we had to live through. You know, the strange thing about this was that when I went to Southside High School (the newly integrated white high school), this unfair practice stopped because the majority of my teachers were white and the few black teachers that I had were noble and fair.

Chapter 25 My Sophomore Year at Southside High

This was my first year to attend Southside High School. My sister Sanguretta had finished and moved to California. I was now the last sibling from Lee Earnest and Patsy Lee, left in a house with my father, stepmother, stepbrother and stepsister, and my brothers through my father, Leelin, Jacob, and Luke. Now it was time to face a new challenge—that of going to a predominately white school. As I rode on the bus with other black kids from surrounding neighborhoods, many of us were talking, wondering what this experience would be like.

We wondered if we would be treated fairly and with respect. It had not been too long before that when my sister had had a major confrontation with a racist teacher at Southside. Would we face the same fate? Would we be isolated and attacked? Would we be allowed to be in the same class with the white students? Would we be able to compete with or against them? Would there be justice for us when the time came for justice to be exercised? Other kids just wished that this was all just a bad dream and that things could just be the way that they used to be.

As we got off the bus at Southside High School, we noticed that the better buses were used to pick up the white kids and that all of the black kids were getting off the older, less-maintained buses. Later this proved to be a disturbance that had to be dealt with through the principal's staff. I am sure that they were staring at us as we were staring at each other, as if waiting for some advantage to overtake us.

We all went inside to the auditorium so that we could be briefed on school rules, etc. Some of the white kids immediately began to threaten us, but we stayed in groups together. There were also some pleasant white kids who smiled at us and made conversation. As time went by, the tension subsided; there were still some problems and a few fights, but progress was being made.

I really excelled in my classes, especially the sciences and math. Many of the white kids desired to study with me. I had no problem with that, but some of my black friends did; they felt as if I was betraying them, but I tried to explain to them that we could all learn together and that this was what Dr. Martin Luther King Jr. meant and would want us to do. Some accepted this, while others didn't.

At the end of each year, awards were given out for each class subject. Many of the teachers, black and white, acknowledged my accomplishments by awarding me with the yearly awards in algebra, science, and history, and my name was mentioned as a candidate for the other classes. This was a big deal at that time because the name of recipients of these awards would be put in the newspaper.

I was approached by sponsors of the student council and a few of my new white friends and was asked to join the student council. The student council was very powerful at Southside and was responsible for a good part of the leadership, which fell between staff and student body. They had a budget and more money than all of the other clubs put together. They were a mini-government ready and willing to exercise the law on behalf of anyone who felt like a victim. They were also the voice of the students mixed with the voice of the teachers, trying to bring about change, when needed, to accommodate all.

Surprising, my father was all in favor of it. At first I thought that he was giving his approval because this was something that I was interested in, but later I found out that a bunch of white people who lived nearby were saying what a great student and leader I was. This was the factor that lead my father to say, "You outta work in that thang with them." I accepted a position as chaplain and parliamentarian.

Within the first week of my being a member, we had a huge racial issue. It was homecoming week and girls were raising money. The girl who raised the most money would be homecoming queen, and runners-up would be those girls with the next highest amount. The amount of money that each girl turned in was supposed to be confidential in the student council (the student council sponsored homecoming), but the president and other officials leaked information that a black girl had the most money.

Some of the white student council members then began putting money into the next runner-up white girl's fund. Other blacks who were seniors in the student council caught this. I really didn't get involved but mostly observed. There were blacks complaining to me, telling me that as the parliamentarian,

I should take action. Then there were the whites coming to me telling me about how a bad situation just got worse and out of control. I then thought, *I don't need this* and turned in my resignation to the sponsoring teachers. When others in the student council heard of this, they resigned as well. Therefore, the sponsors took action and put the president and many officials on probation from student council activities. They had to do something because there were threats and fight all over the school. Things were very chaotic and out of control.

Dealing with the student council was not enough, and all members and those who had quit were brought back into a meeting with the principal and student council sponsors (Mr. Optiman and Mr. Ford). From that meeting, it was decided that there would be two homecoming queens that year and that the new student council officers for the next year would put steps in place to prevent this type of problem from happening again.

At this time, Mr. Optiman, who was also my physics teacher, stated that those who had resigned should stay on so that we could change the problems that were in the current system. He asked me first to come back and work in the student council, and I accepted, as others did after me. It took some time for the scars of this uproar to pass, but it did pass.

A few months later, it was time to start getting ready for the Christmas float in the Selma Christmas parade. We had a few racial issues, but due to earlier problems with homecoming, we were able to work them out.

Chapter 26 You Can't Have It Back

*I*t was my junior year at Southside High School. The sophomore year was completed and I had been inducted into Honor Society (average of 3.5 or better) and had made great strives to help with racial issues and tension at Southside. The summer had gone by when I worked in the fields most of the time. The work had been long, hard, and very strenuous, with only my stepbrother to help sell the crops. (He had a thing against hard work; more like an allergy.) After completing work on the farm for the summer, I took off to spend a few weeks in Pensacola. Crops had produced longer than normal that summer, so I only had about three and a half weeks left.

Things had changed quite a bit in Pensacola. Rosaline stayed next door, but the word was that she no longer liked boys. Some of the boys that I played basketball with had moved, and a few others had been put in juvenile detention. Some of the fellows from Tate had graduated, so many of the players were new to me.

We played and struck up new relationships, and things were getting back to the way they used to be. Back home, I had spent hours into the night shooting hoops in the goal on the back of that old pecan tree. So my touch was still there, even through the mist of cucumber blisters and scratches from pulling plants for market; I could still find the perimeter with great accuracy and consistency. Since I was short, my key shots were hook shots with the left hand mostly but with the right also, fade-away jump shots and the long shot outside twenty feet from any spot. I loved to compete against others and refused to be stopped just because of my size. It didn't take long for me to get respect on the court back in Pensacola.

Girls who were watching now seemed to be interested in getting sexually involved much more than I was willing to be or ready for. I was a virgin and planned to hold out. I learned not to tell this to the opposite sex. As I met and struck up relationships with these girls, that question of sex eventually became the topic of discussion. Some girls were excited by learning this and others dropped me like a hot potato.

So I learned not to talk about it with them. When the situation would present itself with a girl, I would play along to a certain point. I would then tell the girl that the time was not right and follow up with "Let's take our time" or "You don't have to do this for me to care about you" or "You are special and this requires a special moment for you" or "I just got out of a bad relationship." These expressions seemed to interest them even more, and many of them would ask, "Where are you from again?"

This was easy because none of those girls were Becky Ann. Becky Ann had changed. She had a boyfriend now, and even though she would tell me that they were just friends, it was not the same between us anymore. Becky Ann said that she cared the same for me, but I just couldn't believe her.

One night she called me and we talked. She finally admitted that they were a couple and until my arrival had been serious. So I asked her, "Why are you calling me?" The reply was that she wanted us to be together. I replied that three is a crowd and that she couldn't have both of us. She told me that she would break up with him to be with me.

We were a couple again, and it was already into my last week there. We were at a block party and we left early and went back to my brother's house for a few minutes. In the middle of making out, she told me that she was still seeing the other guy. This beat all; I told her, "How can you be here with me now?" The reply was that she loved me and that I was not around enough. She said that we should just enjoy the time that we had, but I wasn't in agreement with that. I wanted to ask Becky Ann if she was sexually active with the other guy, but I just did not want to know the answer, because deep down inside I already knew. In either case, I know that I was not ready for such a thing.

So in the middle of the private, one-on-one time with Becky Ann, with tears in my eyes, I said, "It's time for you to go home." She kissed me, wiped the tears from her cheeks, and said, "No! I want to be here with you." But I told her, "How could you when you belong to someone else? I can't share you with others." I walked with her back to the block party all hugged up, but I didn't feel close, just abandoned.

I left Pensacola a little bit sad and started my junior year at Southside. My father still restricted me from playing any sports. A few months later, I got a letter from Becky Ann. In it she stated how much she really missed the times that we had, especially early on when we first met. I was thinking, *Okay, that's great,* but as I read on, I learned that she was seeing yet another guy different from the one she had told me about and that she was pregnant. She stated that the father wanted to break up with her and she felt all alone. I really hated to see this happen to her, and in a letter back to her, I replied, "Life is not over. Do the right things, pick up the pieces, and continue to live."

I realized then that others were changing around me, but that I was still staying in the safety shell. Some said that others were growing up and that I was still naïve and probably still believed in the tooth fairy. Looking back now, we chose different paths; my path was just a little more conservative.

Even classmates at Southside had changed during the previous year. Many were into deep relationships that were producing offspring, but I, still innocent of such things, loved the idea of having a girlfriend, but when faced with choices, I would take playing football or basketball first any day. All of those things took a back seat to academics and leadership activities (mostly by my father's choice).

By the second year, I had a reputation and was called the "professor" by my peers and all those who sought help with schoolwork. Not only that, but I also made the mistake of being labeled a nice guy. This is a killer title for any man who wants to ever have a girlfriend, because in general, girls at this age don't like nice guys for boyfriends. The best you can be is a close friend, which stinks because a girl is more likely to date a guy that she totally dislikes and thinks is repugnant than date you (her close friend). The girls seemed to like the dogs and in many cases, it didn't matter what kind. Just as long as he was a dog was the important thing. Why is this? It's really simple. When a guy gets, "You are a nice friend," it means you are not looked upon as a normal, functional male anymore but as some sensitive friend who is neither male nor female; you have entered the Twilight Zone of dating. The best that I could hope for was to find some girl who did not see me that way or did not know me and start over (and try not to be such a nice guy).

Well, my popularity was too great for my own good. I had a great reputation for helping others with their homework and providing them good counseling advice. Even if I tried to be close to a girl, they would hug me and say something to me like, "You are so sweet. Don't you ever change. I hope that we can always be friends." It just looked like they were all growing up and I was stuck in my younger years being that same old sweet guy.

I was now old enough to work in Selma and ended up working in the Yellow Front Supermarket, which was located on Water Avenue. It was the last street before the Alabama River. Most of the black people we knew had shopped at Yellow or Washington Street supermarket. For many these had been the only supermarkets that they could shop at during the days of Jim Crow laws when there were white-only establishments. The owners were always white, and often the food was not of the same quality as was found in other supermarkets, but it did my father good to have his sons work in this store.

So I started working there every Friday after school until closing and all day Saturday from 8:00 a.m. to 6:00 p.m.

I saved up enough money to buy a phone for the house and made a deal with my dad that I would get it installed if he paid the bill. I proved to him that the bill would never be more than fifteen dollars per month. I stressed to him that he would have his own telephone in the house and would not have to go to other people to have them make phone calls and that he would not have to depend on the white landowner giving him urgent and important family messages. I told him that all of his children and family would be able to call his number and speak to him very easily.

I was surprised when he said, "Go ahead and do it." The cost for this was around 106 dollars, which I had saved up by not buying anything for Christmas that year. I had the phone service installed and on the same day arranged for my older brothers to call my dad. I believe my father was proud of me that day, as I heard him tell my older brother, "Pop will work to get what he wants."

I continued to save most of what I made except for paying people to drop me off at home after work. Even though my father had two old cars, he would not allow me to use either to go to work in. I would always ride with him and my stepmother to town but would have to find a way to get home. This worried me greatly because many times I didn't know how I was going to get home. I lived approximately ten miles from Selma in Sardis, and if I had to walk, I most certainly had to cross the Edmond Pettus Bridge, which stretches across the Alabama River. This was the same place where racist whites, policemen, and the like had forced many blacks off the bridge and released dogs on them, and water hoses were used (Bloody Sunday). The thought of having to walk across this bridge late in the evening brought great fear to me. Not only that, but I also had a fear of heights.

I only remember not finding a ride home two times. I had called home and asked my father if he would come and get me, but he refused. On one occasion, I was walking toward the bridge and some classmates from school picked me up and dropped me off for a few dollars.

The other time, I had to walk. The sun was going down when I started out, and it was raining slightly. I can remember bowing down on my knees before crossing the bridge and praying to God for strength: strength to face my fears—not just face them but overcome them and not fall into the river. I didn't know how to swim either. As I ended my prayer, I felt a burden lifted and it was as if all those who had given their lives for equality in Selma, Alabama, and surrounding areas were there with me. We marched across the Edmund Pettus bridge, singing "We Shall Overcome."

After crossing over the bridge, I felt a great deal of accomplishment but looking ahead, I still had about 10 miles to go before making it home. As I started the 10-mile walk from the end of the bridge, I began to think of how this trial was indicative of life's true journey; that major obstacles are huge from appearance, but after conquering them, the level of performance required to finish or complete a task is major.

After forty minutes, the rain began to pour and I started to pick up my step by jogging. There was no road for me to jog on and pedestrians didn't have the right of way in Sardis/Selma, especially black pedestrians. So for a good part of the way, you can say I jogged off-road, in mud and grass. I was angry with my father for not helping me, angry with myself for working there.

161

I wanted to give up but could not. Despite the conditions at home, they were worse being a young black man out in the dark jogging down a heavily traveled road. I don't know how many cars passed by me, making fun of me, both blacks and whites, but only whites yelled out the window, "Stupid nigger. Don't you know it's raining?" or "You f*&^% nigger" or "mother *&^^%," etc. You get the picture. As bad as you might think, I am glad that no one stopped.

About an hour and a half later, I was only about one and a half miles from home, very tired and thirsty, and right in front of the graveyard of the White Southern Baptist Church in Sardis. I heard noises from the graveyard, regained myself, and began to jog again. Finally home was within sight, so about two hundred yards from home, I began to walk so that no one would think that I was afraid or out of breath.

When I got in the house, my dad started yelling at me, asking me where I had been. After he finished, I told him that I could find no ride home and had to walk all the way home. He knew that I was afraid of the Edmund Pettus Bridge and asked me, "You crossed that bridge?" I then said, "I had to get home, but the Lord was with me every step of the way. I am no longer afraid." He then looked at my clothes and saw that I was soaking wet, muddy, and exhausted. He then told me that I should not do stupid things like that. I asked him what else I could do. He then got really mad with me and started the verbal attack, which lasted for about a half hour. It hurt me, but what else could I do?

Chapter 27 Blessed or Cursed

*I*t was in the fall of my junior year on a Saturday morning. I had just gotten my driver's license a few months earlier. I had been driving for years, but all my driving had been restricted to farming and tending to crops. Well, now I was driving legally, but only to places that my father commanded me to go. We had gone to town, Selma, to purchase a few groceries. My stepmother's brother, Wilson, would always go with us into town. He would hitch a ride to our house and tag along with the rest of the family.

Wilson was married and had a few kids. He and his family lived deeper in the countryside. Like a ritual, he purchased groceries but would also purchase alcohol and indulge, and whenever possible, he would chase women and girls; age just didn't seem to matter.

On this Saturday morning, the weather was extremely bad, with high winds and rain. After we had returned from Selma, my father told me to take Wilson home. I asked him, practically begged him, to let me wait until the rain stopped, but my father thought that I was being disrespectful and shouted some indecent insults my way, finishing by telling me, "Boy, go on and git yo butt out of here and do what I say."

Every bone in my body was against going out and driving in the rain; I just had a bad feeling, but I knew that it was hopeless trying to tell my father anything.

So I took the old work car as I was told. The other old car that my father had was much better for this type of weather because the tires were better and it had power steering and good working windshield wipers. It was raining very hard and I could hardly see, but I was able to get Wilson to his house with no trouble. I then started back on my way home. I had gotten to the last mile when the trouble started.

I came around the corner, saw another truck coming, and could not tell if the other truck was on my side or not. I tried to go over to the right as much as possible, but I overcompensated a little too much. I went off the side of the road and down the banks of a small cliff and flipped over a few times. We had no seatbelts in those days; all I could do was ask God to take care of me. When the car finally stopped and rested upside down, I heard a fire-truck siren and someone calling out to me.

I remember thinking how quick that response was and that the accident had just happened, and then I thought that God was really listening and that maybe everything would be all right. The firemen broke the glass and helped me out; they checked my vitals and cleaned away some blood from a cut on my hand. I was very stressed and they told me that I should be glad to be alive. I then told them that I wished I had died rather than have to face my father. They told me that if my father were a godly man, he would have to be thankful to God that I was not seriously hurt. These great firemen said that they would take me home and talk to my father, and for the first time in my life, I felt safer being in the company of the white man than my own father.

When we got to my house, it was still pouring down. The firemen told my dad that I was lucky to be alive and that somebody must have been looking out for me. My dad yelled at me, saying, "Where is my damn car? You done went and had an accident 'cause you didn't wanta go in the first place." As he continued to yell insults at me, he told me to go inside the house and he said a few more words to the firemen and they were gone. Next, my dad came into the house, yelling, screaming, and cursing me.

In the midst of it all, he accused me of having the accident on purpose and said that I did it because I didn't want to go anyway. Once again, my stepmother was silent. So once again, I took the brunt of my father's wrath—the cursing, the yelling and shouting, spiritually and mentally beating me down. I had just about two hundred dollars that I had been saving up, which I offered to him, but he just keep on insulting me, cursing me, and making me feel smaller and smaller. I remember him saying, "I don't want your God*&*^* money. You all ways messing **&*%^% things up." This went on and on and on.

It didn't stop the next day or the next week, and he continued belittling me, even embarrassing me in front of people at church and at school; anywhere he could, he took the opportunity to hurt me or make me feel worthless.

There wasn't much that I could do. I called each one of my brothers and sisters and begged each of them to let me come and stay with them, but each of them refused. This really hurt even more. I had no outlet to turn to, and though I was blessed to be alive, I was cursed to be in my father's house at this time. I became an alien in my own home, a stranger to all those around me and withdrawn. There were no doctors for me to see, no psychologist or psychiatrist to help me; it was just me alone. I was cursed to obey his every command and yet endure his belittling of me when he felt like it or for his amusement.

I wondered why he felt he had to continuously do this to me. The knife was already in; why did he have to keep on twisting it? I then thought that I should have died in the car accident and that no one would have really missed me or cared about my existence. During this time, I thought about just ending my life. I was miserable and my body had become very numb to pain, whether verbal or physical.

When I went to school, most of the black kids who knew about it (even those who were my so-called friends, except for the Mims family and a good friend named Janice) made jokes and made fun of me. They even joked about how my father was making fun of me, but a majority of the white classmates that I had associated with had great compassion for me. Many of them looked on with disbelief as my so-called soul brothers and sisters ripped me apart. Daisy, Joy, Carlton, and a few others stood up for me along with Angie Mims, Jacob Mims, and Janice. They really cheered me up many days, but the agony of facing this at school and at home wore me down.

Things got so bad that I found myself thinking of ways to end it all. I had let myself slip to a dark place of depression where no one should ever travel. I was considering suicide. My father had treated me so badly that I could not forgive him; you know, it's so hard to love someone and not forgive them at the same time, but I could not forgive him. I was angry with my blood sisters and brothers because no one would let me come and live with them. I was sick of my ignorant so-called black friends who unjustly ridiculed and made fun of me during the worst moments of my life. There was no one for me to seek comfort from. I thought, *What's the purpose of living? If this is it, count me out.* It had been a few months since the accident, but for me, it was like reliving it every day for the past few months.

Even though I was thinking about suicide, I was also praying and asking God to make my life better, to help me face the next day and to help me feel good again. One day, in the hall at school, I accidentally ran into a girl, Lizzy. She was a sophomore and did not know anything about my problems, but she knew of me through my work in the student council and other leadership activities around the school. Lizzy was kind to me and said that we should talk later after school.

At the end of school that day, I met Lizzy at her locker and walked her to the bus. She was really interested in me and said that she would like to talk to me more, so she gave me her number so that I could call her that night. That night, I called her and asked her up front if she had a boyfriend, and for the first time in a few months, I felt excitement and anticipation. She responded by saying that she was in the process of breaking up with her boyfriend, and I told her "that is good enough for me" and asked her if she thought there was a chance for us. She replied in a laughing voice (with sisters in the background trying to get in on the conversation), "What do you think?" I just simply replied, "You know it."

This was start of me leaving my depression behind; no more talk of suicide or looking at the negative aspects of life. So we became a couple around the school, and for the first time I began to visit a girlfriend on Wednesday and Sunday nights. I would have to get a ride with some other guy that would be visiting his girlfriend, but I would always make a deal with the driver to pay for gas.

It seems that the joking and harassing of the car accident stopped after my relationship with Lizzy started, but maybe it didn't. I think knowing that I had someone who would be there for me—a real friend, someone that would fight for me, share, and listen to me even on those bad days and unthinkable events—made all the difference in the world. I believe that God heard my prayers and, through others, delivered me from my demon. By the end of the year, my father stopped belittling and rubbing the accident in my face. He even offered to let me borrow the car sometimes to go and visit Lizzy. I then realized that I had been severely tested and tried and had gone through one monster of a tribulation, and I was afraid of how close I came to failing. I then got a thought that failure and success both sit at opposite ends of a bench and that I sat in the middle.

Chapter 28 Called to Lead

*T*his marked my senior year of high school at Southside. I had maintained an A average and received more awards for academics and leadership than anyone else had received at the school. I had won the student council election to become the first black student council president in school history; this was a big deal in the Selma area at that time, so the local Selma newspaper did a feature on the event. I was on several radio programs to represent Southside High School.

My name and/or picture appeared in the newspaper often, and many of the white people with the power would say good things about me and acknowledge my natural talent for leading and resolving issues between people. They told my dad that he should be very proud of me and my accomplishments, but he still could not give me a pat on the back and say, "Well done, son. You done good." Instead, he ignored giving me any positive feedback for my accomplishments. That didn't stop me from seeking accomplishments. I received awards from the US Army (Honorary Colonel), University of Alabama

(Distinguished Leadership Award), Alabama American Legion (Citizenship Award), American Society of Students (Distinguished Leadership Award), and NAACP (Distinguished Leadership Award).

Many times the white kids would drop me off from school activities and ask me, "Is that where you live?" Most of them had a hard time believing that I was a product of this shotgun house of poverty and yet proved to be so successful in all my accomplishments. I learned that much of who you become is determined by who you think you are and not who others see you as. Despite my poverty, I had finally reached a point of happiness.

My relationship with Lizzy was strong, my academics and leadership were strong, and the students had voted me one of the four "senior favorites" and "most intellectual." But in the middle of all of this, there was more evidence of something that my mother had told me before she died. One night while asleep, I went into a deep dream. I dreamed that I was a preacher. That wasn't the hardest thing to believe, but where I was preaching was very difficult to comprehend. It was at the big white Southern Baptist church on Route 41 in Sardis. A closer look at the dream revealed that there were black people, white people, Indians, and some of other nationalities. It was a strong message for people to come together as one.

When I woke up, I was afraid and excited, and had to tell someone. My father was the first person that I saw. So I began to tell him, but no sooner did I begin to tell him of my dream then he interrupted me and said, "Boy, you ought to stop lying. You ain't got no business lying about thangs like that." I could not understand why he, my own father, would accuse me of lying about something that meant so much to me. My dad appeared to be extremely angry with me, as if I had done something terribly wrong. He even threatened to beat me if I didn't take it back.

But when it came to God, this was one topic that I was never shy to talk about. In the past I had had many aggressive conversations with my dad and other family members. So I considered myself a soldier on the battlefield, refused to take it back, and set off on a course to be heard. My reply to him was that "God has shown me something and I must tell someone about it; I cannot be quiet." When my dad saw how fervent I was about the dream, he was taken with fear and a slight tear or two. Even though he said it was the wind blowing that caused him to tear up, I accredited it to the power of God moving. He just said, "Your stepmother already told me the dream. She had the same dream." And he walked away. No shouts of joy or other emotion; he just simply walked away into the fields. For a minute, I wondered why he wasn't more excited about it, but being overexcited about the dream and by him telling me that my stepmother had the same dream, I immediately began searching for her so that I could hear her tell me what she had dreamed.

I found my stepmother outside and told her my dream; she became nervous and said, "That ain't never happened. How can you and me dream the same thang and on the same night?" For a minute I searched for an answer, and then the words of my belated mother came to me: "God will use you to help others to see." Could this be the time? Was I to dedicate my life to ministering at this time? Was I to go to the big church of the white people in Sardis and tell them? Was I to talk to my pastor about this?

I had no doubt that the message in the dream came from God. Nothing is without cost, though, and when I told Lizzy about it, I noticed a change in her attitude. She told me that she didn't want to spend the rest of her life with a preacher and that she would not have a boyfriend who was in the ministry either. Lizzy put me in a difficult position. I truly did love her, and she had been a rock to help me get over many of my problems. Not only was she my girlfriend but my best friend as well; how could I disappoint her? On the other hand, God had always been there for me through the hardships of losing loved ones, living in a white-supremacy-dominated society, and living through poverty.

I would love to tell you that I made the right decision, but I didn't. Whatever the message from the dream that my stepmother and I had was, I put it on the back burner and chose to get closer to Lizzy. Deep inside my soul, I knew what it meant. I knew that this was what my mother had spoken of early on in my life. I knew that it meant that my life was for Christ and that I was chosen by Him to speak for Him, but I decided that I was not willing to give up Lizzy. So I decided to go to the University of Alabama (UA, home of the Crimson Tide, in the shadows of the mighty Bear Bryant). I also had offers to go to other schools, such as Purdue, Auburn University, Alabama A & M, Gramlin State, and West Point Academy in New York, but I was more concerned about staying near Lizzy. I was guilty of making her an idol and based too much on our relationship. This was one of the worst mistakes that I ever made in my life and I would reap the pain from it later. At the time, it seemed as if God was just going to let me slide.

Chapter 29 Entering a New World

I received leadership scholarships and student loans and had a job in the work-study program to cover my expenses at the university. This community was like nothing that I had ever seen. I arrived a week early for freshman orientation and learned the basics about the campus and its programs.

I was invited to go to a fraternity party; they had even promised to have an escort date for me if I planned to attend. I mentioned this to members of the African American Association (AAA) at the university, and they assured me that it was a white fraternity. Nowadays you may think that this was no big deal, but in the heart of Dixie, it was still an issue. We as people still did not live as one America, and the thought of black boys being with white girls was not appreciated much either. The AAA gave me information on the fraternity and also told me about Confederate Day. This was a Saturday picked in Tuscaloosa when white people celebrated their confederate heritage. One event was a parade that depicted the old South and included portraying black people as slaves on the floats.

The fraternity that invited me and had provided me with a southern belle date was a big sponsor of these activities. The AAA wanted me to go and see if they would let me in and follow through on providing me a date, but I didn't want to go. I did want to champion the cause of equality, but thought that I would be betraying Lizzy, my girlfriend. So I decided not to go.

I found my dorm room in Petty Hall and was greatly impressed. There were community showers and bathrooms for groups of dorm rooms, and each room had a phone in it. The cafeteria was downstairs, and one could eat as much as one pleased at mealtime. There were two game rooms downstairs, each with a big TV, and there were basketball courts in the back of the dorm. My activity fees included tickets to all sporting events and some health insurance.

I thought to myself that I could really get used to this. After all, it was nothing like the place that I came from; I even felt a little guilty being there in such a nice place. Life was good until my roommate arrived. He was a white guy who enjoyed having girls, alcohol, and smoking, even the bad cigarettes. It didn't matter whether I was in the room or not, he did what he was going to do with his company anyway.

One time I remember going to my room and seeing my roommate with two girls on his bed, and there were white girls on my bed too and they were all smoking pot. They asked me if I wanted to come and join them. All kinds of thoughts were going through my mind. I didn't drink or smoke, but should I have been sociable without doing those things? I was still a virgin as well, but maybe we could just talk, I wondered. The bigger concern was that they were white and I was black. I knew of many stories of black people being taken advantage of and unjustly accused and punished for crimes that they did not do or being punished for being black. Earlier that year a black teenager had been hanged in Mobile for dating a white girl and another was hanged in Monroeville because a black young man had had sex with a white girl. There were reports on the news that black men were being hanged and beaten for just looking at or whistling at white women. All of these thoughts entered my mind at this time. I did what the culture demanded by refusing to have anything to do with them and told them that they should not be doing that in my room. There were many things wrong with that picture, and I didn't know if this was part of a trick or not, but I knew that it wasn't for me. I asked them to leave, turned on the lights, and began studying.

I didn't know what was going to happen next but thought that I would rather get beaten up right then than get thrown out of school and humiliate my family for something stupid like this. I knew that there were many white people back home just waiting for my failure. The girls got off and out of my bed and said, "We should go." My roommate and the girls in his bed grabbed their bottle and began to leave and said a few remarks on the way out that I tuned out. Later that week, my roommate did apologize and told me that I needed to loosen up and have some fun. I told him that I didn't smoke or drink and that I wasn't into sex and that I was still a virgin. He then said, "Have you ever seen a *Playboy*?" I replied by saying, "What's that?" He found this very funny and showed me a collection of them. He picked one and gave it to me. I must admit this was exciting to me, and I posted the centerfold on the wall beside my bed. Since I didn't have to worry about my parents visiting me or any girls, I had no pressure to take it down.

There were a few thousand black students who attended the university, which made up a black community within the university. Within the second month, my roommate was gone. I don't know what happened to him, but I had a room to myself for the rest of the semester. I had made friends with a group of other blacks from Evergreen, Buddy and Doug (who introduced me to an endless list of others from the Evergreen area), Sean P., Phillip, and JD. These guys were my best friends. I was the only one who had a room by myself for the rest of the first semester, so they would often come over to play cards and talk about the college experience.

One time Buddy brought his girlfriend over, and she didn't say anything about the picture, but I know it disturbed her. This alone did not make me take it down. I did something dumb that lead me to that point. A few of the guys from Evergreen kept telling me that Beverly (another student from Evergreen) was interested in me, so even though I was committed to Lizzy back home, I thought, *Why not check it out and see?* After all, Lizzy and I were both still virgins. These guys told me that they would tell me what to say. So I called Beverly one night with all the guys in the room, and one of the guys told me to just ask her for it. I then asked him, "What do you mean?" He said, "You know—it." I said something to Beverly, that I am still ashamed of today. I said, "Beverly, give up the rump!" She asked me what I said and I was fool enough to say it again. She told me that I was crazy and hung up. Then Buddy's girlfriend called and asked to speak to him; she knew right away that he had something to do with it. Well, in my room, all the guys were cracking up, but I felt like I had been the brunt of a foul joke. The next day, every girl from the Evergreen circle who saw me laughed in my face and said, "Give up the rump!" Girls even from Stillman College, a black college on the other end of town, called me and said, "Give up the rump!" After about two days of this, I went to my room and destroyed the *Playboy* picture that hung on my wall.

Later on, the guys and I were at the university theater to see a movie. We went to see our first X-rated movie. We did not understand the full impact of an X rating, but it didn't take long to see what it meant. I was amazed at what I had seen and heard. I spoke to others about this movie because I just could not believe that people were doing that on screen. I had grown up with this innocence and thought that everyone was a Christian, at least to some degree. Well, I was soon discovering that there was a whole world out there and that my views and understanding were just one seed of many. Some asked me if I was just hatched out of an egg, and others said that I must have lived a sheltered life. This was just the start of being exposed to the world outside of Sardis, Alabama. Whatever you were looking for, it could be found on campus.

I found this to be a time of great discovery and was challenged daily about my beliefs. All of my college friends were black and shared the same beliefs for the most part, but we were all challenged to the max to hold on to our morals, convictions and faith.

On Sundays, many of us would go to church together. One Sunday, a group of us black students headed off to a Southern Baptist church on the outskirts of campus. When we got there, we were told that we could not go in and would have to leave. This reminded me very much of Sardis because white people did not allow black people to come to their place of worship. (Some god they served!) The AAA took action right away and contacted the local chapter of the NAACP. The NAACP got in touch with the national chapter and Jesse Jackson. Leaders from all over the country began to prepare to come and support actions to be taken against the Southern Baptist church. This became national news, and before the week was over, the church offered an apology and asked us to return the next Sunday. Many of the national leaders and students went, but I refused to go back because we were only being invited due to the pressure and visibility that the Southern Baptist church was receiving. Instead I went to the local African Episcopal Methodist church, where I knew I would have a spirit-filled experience.

The end of my first year came and I passed all my courses. I even made the dean's list, which caused my picture and accomplishment to be posted in the local newspaper in Selma. The people that my dad worked for showed it to him, which made him proud. (He never told me he was proud, but just the fact that he told me about it was an indication that he was proud.) When I went home, I went by Yellow Front Supermarket, the place where I had worked while in high school, and I saw the owners. They said, "We were shocked to see your picture in the newspaper." They spoke this very fast and tried to say that they didn't mean anything by it, but I replied, "You don't think a black person can be as smart as a white person, do you?" They then said that wasn't what they meant. I was getting ready to ask them what they meant, but my dad elbowed me and said, "Time to go."

On the way home, my father lectured me on pushing things. It was his opinion that I should have taken their statements as compliments or just not reacted negatively, the way that he perceived that I had. "Why can't you just let it go?" he asked me. I replied in this case, as I had done on previous occasions, "I just can't let it go."

The following fall, life was quite different. I had worked during the summer to buy my first car—an old Volkswagen hatchback. Lizzy had graduated from high school and moved to Tuscaloosa to attend Stillman College, a private black college about ten miles from the University of Alabama. At the start of the fall year, I gave her a promise ring, and the plan was to get married after college. Life was good; there were all the activities of college life and nice living quarters, the person that I planned to spend the rest of my life with was just ten miles away, and I had good transportation. All of the gang was back from the previous year, and Alabama was headed for another football bowl game.

I was majoring in math and computer sciences with an average of 6 hours of study per day. This wasn't too bad because I was always able to study a few hours a day on the work-study program. Calculus was the hardest, and I spent on average four hours a day on it, seven days a week.

As the school year drew to a close, I finished with dean's honorable mention, and my relationship with Lizzy was stronger than ever, or so I thought, but one night we were together, she told me that she wanted to date another guy at Selma University (one of the Spartans). I asked her how she could want to go out with someone else if we were planning to be married. She kept insisting that they were just friends, so I told her to do what she thought was best.

Well, she bought a new evening gown, went to the beautician, and went through all the extra motions to go to the ball with this other young man. It was hard for me, but I did my best to trust her. I called her late that night many times, and finally around 1:00 a.m. she returned my call and was very happy. Initially, I thought that she was happy to talk to me, but as I listened to the conversation, I could tell that the Lizzy that I knew was changing to one that I didn't. Then again, maybe she was being who she really was and the previous three and a half years, she was pretending to be someone who really cared about me. In either case, I was very naïve and tried to think on the positive side.

During my junior year, Lizzy had this great need to join Zeta Phi Beta sorority. I, of course, took this to mean that she wanted to be closer to her frat buddies and was totally against the idea. She even had the president of Zeta Phi Beta call me, yelling at me, saying that I shouldn't stand in her way. I told her that Lizzy had a mind of her own and that while she asked for my opinion, she certainly did not honor it all the time. It was only a few years earlier that Lizzy had given me a choice: her or life in the ministry.

There was no rest from Lizzy trying to convince me that sorority life was the way to go. So finally, she got me to commit to join Phi Beta Sigma (brother fraternity to Zeta Phi Beta). After I got on the pledge line, Lizzy was given some startling news: she had been sick and had major surgery earlier during the year and was turned down by the Zeta Phi Beta pledge-line committee.

Our relationship really took a turn for the worse, and it was like her anger was taken out against me. I had sacrificed much for her and to be with her. I even sold my car to help her get needed medicines, etc. It was tough, but we were still together.

While pledging I began to have problems in some of my key courses. My problems were a combination that included, a disconnect between sisters and brothers, problems with my relationship with Lizzy, and the constant grilling of Greek life and its history with respect to the black fraternities and sororities. And then there was the issue of stepping. Each night, seven nights a week, we practiced stepping for hours. As we would see other blacks around campus, many would attempt to find out from us what all the noise was that they would be hearing from the Sigma house when they passed by. But like monks, we were sworn to secrecy and not allowed to speak without the "big brothers'" permission. This was not my nature (to be in a slave role to anyone), and many times I thought about Lizzy and how I had gotten myself into this mess. She wanted to pledge so bad but could not, and I was trapped there because of her. I thought that she would pledge the next semester, and that was the only reason I stayed on line pledging.

Finally "hell week" came. Hell week is normally the last week of pledging and the most difficult. Pledges normally don't sleep during this week, and if they are smart, they hide out when possible. Big brothers and sisters would come in from out of town just to wreak havoc on unsuspecting pledges.

During this time, I had a dream one night. It was after 2:00 a.m. when I got to my dorm room, and I went straight to bed when I got there. That night I dreamed that I was shooting basketball on the court behind my dorm and immediately a storm rolled in and there was great darkness. I fell down, and when I tried to get up, there was a strong hand on my shoulder. I looked behind me and could not make out the face, but He had a white robe on and pointed to the backboard of one of the basketball goals. As I focused on the backboard, I saw the history of the Bible being played out before my very eyes. There was a summary of the events from the Old Testament and the New Testament, including some of the events from Revelation. Toward the end, things were quite bad on the Earth and the feeling was that we were all doomed. Still within the dream, I felt great fear and sadness all over and within my body. I tried to look at the owner of the hand that was on my shoulder, but His hand pointed to the backboard again. I then saw Jesus on the cross and could hear Him say, "You remember me," and the One behind me said, "Will you serve me?"

When I awoke, I was totally wet from sweat and totally worried. I knew that God was knocking, and I was not willing to open the door. Once again, God was reminding me of His calling, but I remained distant from that purpose. That Friday night I crossed over and became a full brother of Phi Beta Sigma fraternity. There were the members of a campus Christian Bible study group that came out to congratulate me, along with Lizzy and a good number of other friends. Pledging was over, and I was free to live the life of a fraternity man, but the dream that I'd had a few nights earlier was still on my mind. Lizzy didn't want to hear anything about it, and I dared not tell any members in the Bible study about it.

The college Greek life became a part of me and quite often, we participated in community service programs, many parties, and Greek step shows. This was back-home stepping in the South by us Sigmas, Alphas, Q-dogs, and Kappas. It was a part of our routine, and anytime we sponsored a party, we would step at the end of the party. Each pledge line was responsible for picking a line name that would be shared by everyone on the line. The name that my line picked was "Gator." My new name became C-Gator, and my line brothers took on new names, A-Gator and D-Gator. We even had blue-and-white IZOD gator shirts to wear when we stepped. The name Gator stuck after we became fully pledged members, and all the other brothers began to pick a name using the Gator reference. There was Tata-Gator and Be-Gator, M-Gator and Sir Gator, G-Gator, and T-Gator, and the list goes on. I was the originator of the name Gator, so none was as popular as the name C-Gator, which probably led me into much trouble. Many girls would ask, "Why do they call you C-Gator?" There were always rumors floating around about fraternity names, and I would always seize and ride the wave of each rumor, thereby making the name C-Gator even more exciting.

As time led me to my senior year, things were really different with Lizzy. I noticed that she was accusing me of cheating on her and constantly telling me of rumors that she was hearing about me. When she first came to Tuscaloosa, we were inseparable, but now we were seeing each other only two or three times per week. I noticed that she began to talk about other guys quite a bit. At first I thought that she was trying to make me jealous, but later I learned that there was another reason.

She was angry with me because she was not a Zeta Phi Beta woman and I was a Phi Beta Sigma man. The fact that I had only committed to do this because of her was irrelevant now. The young lady that I loved so dearly now despised me and did not want to spend her life with me, but like many, I did not see this at the time and was still deeply crazy in love with Lizzy. The summer had come, and we both had planned to go to summer school at our respective schools. I was making up two core classes in my major and minor. I had made my first F ever (in my life). It was an advanced computer graphics class, and the instructor did not like me or any other black or minority. I studied with a white guy who had an A average and would compare my notes with his notes all the time, but this didn't help. One day the instructor said to me, "I don't know how so many of you all got in here, but you don't have any business being here. Your writing and grammar is terrible. I don't know how you are going to make it!" Today I wonder what that professor is doing or if he is still discouraging students who don't look like he does. The other class was Advanced Calculus; I had a D in this class that I wanted to make up.

Lizzy had told me that she was coming back to Tuscaloosa a few weeks later, so I never thought anything different until her mother called me and asked me if I had seen her and said that Lizzy had told her that she was going be staying with me. It had been close to a week now, and Lizzy's mother had not heard from her and I didn't know where she was, but I did know that she had lied to me and her mother. Her mother gave me a number that Lizzy had given her some time ago to call if there was an emergency. So I called this number, which was the telephone number of the women's dorm that Lizzy had stayed in, and Lizzy's roommate came to the phone and broke the news to me. She could not bring herself to tell me the whole story. She just told me that Lizzy was staying at with a guy on campus named Lucus. She was crying as she told me this and said, "She has been seeing him for some time now. I wanted to tell you because you don't deserve this." I graciously thanked her for telling me the truth and hung up.

I had sold my car earlier to help Lizzy with some bills and had to get a couple of my frat brothers to take me to where this Lucus lived. I said nothing on the ride to Lucas's place, but my frat brothers were trying to console me. So when we got there, they all stared at the building, but not me. I hopped out the car and had no problem finding the right door. I knocked and Lucus answered the door. He was quite a bit older than me but he knew who I was. I told him that I needed to talk to Lizzy. He said "sure" and went outside. I then looked and saw Lizzy ironing his clothes. I asked her why she was doing this and what had happened to our plans, our future, and being honest with each other. She then yelled a few obscenities at me and said, "I want my stuff that's at your place!" I asked for the ring that I had given her, but she refused to give it back. I then grabbed her and heard my frat brothers calling me. At the same time, I became dizzy and could only see stars floating around in darkness. Suddenly it was becoming very hot in the room, so I stumbled out the building, hearing others say, "Isn't he that C-Gator from U of A?"

I fell outside under a tree, in shock, half-dazed and between a state of consciousness and passing out. After about fifteen minutes, I came back to reality and my frat brothers were there trying to comfort me, but there was no comfort. I was thinking that Lizzy had made a fool out of me and thought back to something that her father had told me some time ago before he died. He had said, "Lizzy is not good enough for you." That statement was never important until this event occurred. Well, I was broken down, and finally one of my frat brothers said it: "C-Gator, there are too many people that look up to you for you to be broken down like this. There are other girls and YOU are C-Gator, so let's go home." So on that note, they helped me off the ground as I took one more look at the building that now had taken my dream girl away.

On the way back, I said nothing and had no expression; I stared deep into the trees, sky, and surroundings. I got to my apartment, and the guys didn't want to leave me and kept asking me if I was going to be all right. I assured them that I would be fine, but they were still concerned. You see, during the spring of that year, two people that we know had committed suicide. One was the pastor at the church on the campus of Stillman College (I had taken a religion course that the U of A offered at Stillman) and the other was a dear friend of mine. I told them that I had to be alone at some point in time anyway but that I might be "beaten right now, spirits down, but I'm not broken. I'm not done fellows."

When they left, I called Lizzy's mother and told her that Lizzy was all right. Then I began to cry as I told her the rest. She always referred to me as "my son." She could not believe what I was telling her, denied it, and said that she was going to get to the bottom of this. I told her that Lizzy and Lucus were packing up and planned to go to Florida. Lizzy's mother cried with me and for me and told me that she would always love me and see me as her son, no matter what Lizzy did with her life. Her mother was special and always treated me like a son. I guess she reminded me in some ways of my birth mother.

That weekend my friend JD (who had recently pledged Kappa) was going home, so I tagged a ride from him to get home for the weekend. JD and I talked about what had happened between me and Lizzy, like many on both campuses were doing. I thought, *Four years plus developing this relationship. Man, I am done with girls!* JD was a good friend; he made a few comments, but he mostly listened to me the whole way home.

My father, stepmother, and kids had moved to another house now. A few of my older brothers had worked to buy an unfinished house that was on a little more than a half acre. It wasn't perfect but was much better than the old shack that didn't even belong to us. My folks always liked JD, so he hung around a few minutes. As JD was leaving, my stepmother asked me how was Lizzy doing. I looked at her and said, "Her mother called, didn't she?" Of course, the answer was yes.

I informed them of what had happened, but they had many questions, which I answered. My dad sat quietly for a few minutes and then said in his loud way, "Boy, I always thought you cared too much for that girl; she didn't deserve it." There it is—from the wisdom of Lee Earnest Coker came my answer. I had cared too much for someone who was not sure about me. I had put God in the background so that she, Lizzy, could grandstand, and now the time had come to pay the consequences. My troubles were just starting.

I spent that weekend feeling sorry for myself, but my dad told me that I should stop being a fool and move on. At the time I thought that was harsh, but it made me toughen up and get ready for Monday. So when I got back to my apartment, I tore up and burned every picture and letter I had of Lizzy. I took all of her stuff that I had to the Sigma frat house and burned it. Some of the members and their girlfriends were there and said, "That's good stuff you are burning," but I said nothing to anyone and sought no permission. I was a man on a mission. I had to do this to feel better. That summer I did terribly in my classes. Lizzy was calling me, asking why I didn't call her to see how she was doing. The surgery that she'd had had earlier was a hysterectomy, but I figured that she had chosen Lucus and dissed me in public like that, so there was nothing else to say. She was even calling me at work a lot. She kept asking for her stuff too. By now all my love had turned to hate and there were no soft spots for girls, especially Lizzy.

As I started my senior year, I was still performing terribly in my classes. I had moved to the Sigma frat house out of my apartment, but because of a few brothers who always tried to take your girl, my search was on for another apartment. There was Priscilla, whom I cared a lot about, but she said that I was still hung up on Lizzy. Then there was Margaret, whom I cared for, and she cared for me, but I allowed myself to be manipulated by a jealous frat brother. Through his crafty plan, I made a pass at one of Margaret's friends, and Margaret was through with me. I don't blame her; she did the right thing. After these events, I just didn't care much about my relationship with girls. I was taking girls' numbers just because I could. I could not concentrate, and my grades were suffering, My personal life was crumbling and my spiritual life was dormant, and C-Gator had changed from being the fun, playful loving guy to a cold-hearted and unconcerned frat boy.

One night I had a dream that I was all alone. I was falling in this deep, deep hole; I was constantly trying to grab the sides, but the more I grabbed, the faster I would fall. Then, out of nowhere, a golden rope was thrown down in the hole. When I reached for the rope, I immediately began to rise to the top. When I got to the top, there were a group of people there waiting for me. I knew these people, but when I awoke I could not remember who they were. But when I went outside to go to class, they came up to me. I was startled because when I saw them, I knew that they were the ones at the top of the hole from my dream. They were members from a campus Bible study that I had occasionally attended. I had other dreams that I refused to tell them about, but this one I told them about. I also confessed to them some of the bad things that I had done and was doing, including an affair with a married lady. I had allowed myself to fall into love with a married woman and she was in love with me. There were times that I was out of things, didn't go to work, had no food or anything, and this special woman took care of all of my needs. Well, all but 1, the most important which would have nullified the relationship. My spiritual life was suffering terrible and I found myself sinking deeper and deeper into it.

All of this I confessed to this Christian group. They listened at all of it and said, "You know what you need to do." So I started the transition of changing back to a fun and loving guy and began to spend more time in the Word, but my relationship with the married woman was still going strong. I even had other girlfriends just to cover up my relationship with the married lady. When I would meet with the Bible group, I would tell them that I was working on improving and that there was a lot to change. They would always tell me to trust my dreams, which meant to trust God.

The end of my senior year had come and I was not going to graduate; by now, I had failed two classes and needed to pass them to graduate. I also had a job offer waiting from Southern Bell if I made a C or better in each of those classes in the summer. As bad as I had been, still willfully sinning, God was still carrying me. Despite my bad grades and my bad habits, this door was still opened for me by the Lord, but the question was whether I would be able to do my part and walk through.

The following summer, I enrolled to take the two courses that I needed to graduate, but I still failed to have the focus needed to pass. At the same time, Lizzy was still trying to make demands of me, even though we had gone separate directions. Since I was beyond the fourth year of school, I had picked up extra jobs to pay for the increased cost of school. The bottom line was that my life seemed wasted; my brother and sisters were all doing well, but I felt like a failure. My grades had suffered greatly, and I had failed to graduate. I had now failed several classes and was on the verge of failing more classes. The lady that I had planned to marry had left me for someone else and embarrassed me greatly, but I think most of all I was out of step with God.

Chapter 30 When I Said Goodbye to My Father

The time was July 1982, and I had gone home for the July 4 holiday. That hot Alabama summer night, I laid down in a hot room with no air conditioning or good air circulation, totally exhausted from my trials and tribulations, many of which I had brought on myself. I began to talk to God by telling him that I was tired and did not have the strength to go on and that if this was it, he should just take my life. However, there was no response from God. As this type of conversation continued, I drifted off to sleep. A few hours later, there was a knocking at the door. I got up and went to see who was at the door.

When I opened the door, there was a shotgun pointing at my chest, and my spirit, soul, and mind could hear the voice of God talking to me and answering my previous question of the night. Plainly, in the spirit, I could hear God saying, "Calvin, you make the choice. If you want to die, just say the word, but Calvin, if you want to live, then just say the word." As of this day,

I do not know what word I said, but I know that I chose to live. So based on my choice, God read my heart and desire. Then he empowered the word that I delivered such that it gave me life. In the midst of all of this, my stepmother fainted and my dad was grabbing his chest.

The man then gave me the shotgun, which I passed over to my father. He then said, "I just killed my daddy." It was my stepmother's brother, the same one who had molested me, my stepbrother and my stepsister and had us doing bad things when we didn't know any better. I then asked several questions about his father. It turns out that he and his mother had been drinking and smoking pot, and his father was asking them to stop. But they took offense to the father's interference and began to threaten him, and things got out of hand. At some point in time, the father hit the mother in the back of the head with a hoe. This caused the son to brutally beat his father and leave him out in the woods somewhere near the house.

I told my stepmother's brother that he needed to turn himself in to the police. After I talked to him for about fifteen minutes, he agreed to talk to the police. I called the sheriff's office, reported the crime, and had him confess all that he had done. One of the deputies guided me through the steps of what to do when we would arrive at the scene and asked me if I thought he was a threat. (He was high.) My father then said that he would stay at the house with my stepmother's brother until the police arrived, but I told him that I needed him to go with me to start looking for the bodies. He said that he would go but that his heart wasn't what it use to be; I thought that was a strange thing for him to say. So a neighbor went with me instead.

The house was similar to the old shack that we had lived in, and when we got there, there were no lights on. The neighbor stayed in the car to await and direct the ambulance and police.

I proceeded to the house with a flashlight, went in, and tried to turn on lights, but none of them worked. As I went into one large room, I could hear the sound of flies buzzing, and then, in the middle of this dark room, a hand grabbed my leg. I cannot explain the fear that I had; it was my stepmother's mother. She was laying in a pool of blood and was bleeding from the back of the neck. I found a cloth that I could use to put on the gash in her neck to stop the bleeding and talked with her for a few minutes. She did not want me to leave, so I could not go and search for her husband. I stayed with her until the paramedics arrived. I then went out with others who had arrived and started searching the woods for the husband. I only stayed there for about another hour and then went back home to tell my stepmother the current state of things.

I was shocked to see that they still had not made the arrest of my stepmother's brother. He rode with me to the hospital to see his mother. While we were there, one of the deputies (the same one I had spoken with on the phone) came to me and said, "You did good tonight." I asked him what was going to happen to my stepmother's brother, and he said that they were going to take him in but not to be surprised if the family did not press charges.

When I got back home, it was about 6:00 a.m. Shortly after that, word came that the father had been found and that he was still alive, so back to the hospital we went. By the time Sunday rolled around, I was still tired. The deputy came by to tell me that he was really impressed with the way I handled myself. All I could tell him was that God was in control of everything and that I was just filling the gaps. A few hours later, Sam (by best friend from college) arrived to give me a lift back to the university. As I was preparing to get into the car, I looked at my father and had a vision that he was in a coffin and floating in a cloud. It was like being in a daze for a minute, and then I remember him asking me if I was all right. I replied yes, but I wasn't all right, because I had seen a sign from God that my father's time was near. Despite all that has been said of his actions, I did love him and I never doubted that he loved me or any of his children. As we (Sam, Angie, and myself) were on our way back to the university, I told them what I had seen. They tried to comfort me by saying that it was probably because of all the actions that had occurred over the weekend and that I was probably just tired. I really appreciated their friendship, but I knew that something stronger was at work and that their friendship would prove to be key to me.

Back at the university, the vision of my father's death weighed heavily on my heart and mind. There was no one that I could talk to who would understand. Nothing had improved for me on the campus. Working with my older brother, John L., I began trying to get transferred to the University of Arizona. John L. lived in Tucson, had attended the University of Arizona, and had good connections. My brother Howard had graduated from the University of Arizona as well. I began the process of withdrawing from the University of Alabama. A few weeks had passed and I was in my apartment on a Friday night while JD, one of my best friends, was giving me a haircut when the phone rang.

I remember telling JD that we shouldn't answer because I knew that would not change the news. I then told JD, "It's my stepmother calling to tell me about my dad." I could not answer the phone; JD answered and looked at me with a startled face and said, "It's your stepmother." I reluctantly took the phone as well as the bad news. My father had been in church at a revival service, praying to the Lord, and had a massive stroke. The people at the church got him to Good Samaritan Hospital as soon as they could.

My stepmother, Gertrude, was crying, and the other kids were crying. I wanted to cry, but knew that I could not cry. I concentrated on something that my father had told me time and time again: "A black man's got to be strong; stop that crying." So I fought to hold back the tears so that I could be strong for the family. I told her that I would be there as soon as I could. JD then said, "We can leave right now," so I told my stepmother that I would be there in a few hours. That's the kind of friend that JD was; I knew he had plans for the weekend, but at that time, his plans didn't matter to him and he put my needs above his plans. When we got to Selma, we stopped at the Good Samaritan Hospital to check the status of my father. This was the same hospital that my mother died in, and I already had a bad feeling.

When I saw my father, I almost fell to my knees because I had never seen him totally weak like that. He was unresponsive. I spoke to the doctor in charge and was given little detail. I then began to complain because I felt that they were just waiting for my dad to die by not doing anything to help him. Yes, he was connected to a few tubes and life support, but nothing else was being done and there was no plan of doing anything else. I requested that my dad be moved to Birmingham or Montgomery, which had the best hospitals in the state, but the staff there accused me of being one of those blacks who had to have white people work on their father. (You see, Good Samaritan was the county hospital and had a majority of black medical staff.) I told them that I didn't care what they thought about me but that my father needed critical care at the moment and I didn't care if the people caring for him were red, green, purple, or blue, I wanted to get my father in the place where he had the greatest chance to survive. I then called my brother Howard, who was a doctor in Las Vegas. After Howard spoke with the attending physician, plans were made to move my dad to Montgomery. I was told that this would take a few hours, so JD and I went to see Gertrude and the kids.

We prayed that we would be strong like black men should be when we got to the house. When we got there, Gertrude met me in the yard. She was exhausted, crying, and in shock. She then told me all that had happened and kept saying, "He was on his knees praying for his children when he just fell over." After a few minutes, I gave her the status of my father. She then told me that I had to be strong and take charge of the situation. I told her that this was for her to do, but she insisted that I take charge. We had a few hours of restless sleep and headed back to the hospital. At the hospital, many of the blacks working there were giving me ugly looks, but I stayed focused and went to the attending physician to get status. Within the hour, my dad was going to be moved to one of Montgomery's finest hospitals, but I knew that the reality of my vision was going to be played out. This didn't keep me from pushing to get the best care possible for my father. JD then spoke with me for a few minutes and said, "I am your friend; call me if you need me. My family will be praying for you and your family." He left, weeping, to go to Greenville to see his parents.

My oldest brother, James, called and said that he was on his way and would go to the house while Gertrude and I went to Montgomery. We stayed in the ICU waiting room for eight hours or more as tests were being done on my father. Finally, late in the afternoon, three doctors came out and took us into a special private room and gave us a detailed status of what had happened and the current status of my father's health. One of the doctors said that my father had had a silent heart attack a few weeks earlier. Gertrude then said that he had been unloading a truck of wood and felt faint and had gone to Good Samaritan but that they didn't find anything and sent him home. Another doctor said that because this was not treated effectively, it created a massive stroke that was unrecoverable. The third doctor said that my father was in a vegetative state and had over 95 percent brain damage. At this time, my stepmother was overwhelmed and burst out crying. I remember embracing her and saying, "We've got to make it; we must hold on."

Next the first doctor said that we should consider signing a "do-not-resuscitate order" and taking my father off life support. Once again my stepmother told me to do what was best. I informed my older sisters and brothers, but the opinions and thoughts from each varied. James, my oldest brother, told me to do what I thought was best because there was no way I could please everybody. I made no decisions on this day (Saturday). Gertrude and I went back home to Sardis, where there were many people in and around the house. They all wanted to know the story and help. Some said, "We heard that you caused some trouble in Good Samaritan," and I replied, "trouble had to come." This was an older lady saying this. She then said that Good Samaritan was the only place blacks could go to get healthcare. There were other people listening, so

I said to her, "I don't mean to be disrespectful, but none of you were there. I have seen my mother die there and now it's my father. Right now, my mind is on him." Then others said, "Leave him alone. He did what many of us ought to be doing." I left the house in my father's old Ford truck to go to a place where I could think and pray. While I was going down a hill on Route 41, the hood flew up and blinded me. I thought that I was going to die, and then I began to think that the family was going to have to bury me and my father, but I prayed and asked God to have mercy on me, and soon I was on level road and the hood fell back down. I pulled over, and all I could do was cry. Later that night, at the house, I had to comfort others. I did not get any sleep, worrying about what to do about the decisions to be made about my dad's health.

Sunday morning we went back to Montgomery and I signed the order to take my father off life support after twenty-four hours. My stepmother asked how could I do that, and I knew that this was hard for her, but I told her that that wasn't him that we saw and that he would not want to live like that. Some of my siblings disapproved, but I gave them the reasoning. We stayed in Montgomery until the afternoon and headed back home. About an hour after being at home, a lady from the hospital called us to tell us that she saw them trying to resuscitate my dad and that they were unsuccessful. A few minutes later, it was confirmed by the hospital in Montgomery that my father, Lee Earnest Coker, was dead.

It was a hard thing for the house to take because my father was the force of the family. It was hard on my stepmother, James and his family, my little brothers and friends, and the neighbors who were there. My older sisters and brothers began to make plans to come for the funeral. I immediately began to get things ready for the funeral (organizing a service and program, getting the grave ready, taking care of burial insurance, etc.). It was very hard to get these things done because my older brother and sisters kept questioning many of the things that I was doing. I remember telling my brother, John L., that I was the one there and that they should respect what I was trying to do rather than ask why all the time. It was stressful for all of them too, but I was not a child either.

Once they all got there, I felt a big sigh of relief. I had not had any sleep for a few days, but when they arrived, I slept for a few hours. I had to go back to the University of Alabama to clear out my apartment and say goodbye to a few people. So I headed back on a Thursday evening and began to clean out the apartment. My roommate had already checked out but failed to do his portion of cleaning the apartment, so I called on my friends—JD, Jacob, Sam, Angie, Jeanne, Buddy and others. They all put time in throughout the day as they could. At about 1:00 p.m., we were mostly done and there was a knock at the door. It was my married friend. We went for a walk around the building and ended up back in the apartment. She was heartbroken that I was sad because she saw the pain that I was in because of my father's death, but she was also saddened because I told her that it was time to break up our relationship and that it just wasn't right. We spent a few more hours together and then my friend Sam said, "All right, C-Gator, it's time to move." I embraced her long and hard as tears were running down her face, and she left sobbing and crying desperately. I was torn with emotion, but Sam and Angie helped me focus because we were on a tight schedule.

Around 6:00 p.m., we were all packed up; I took a final look at the University of Alabama and said goodbye. I was so tired that I could not drive, so Sam took the wheel and guided us home. When I got home, all of my sisters, brothers, aunts, and uncles were there. They also gave me a hero's greeting, and for a few minutes the joy outweighed the sadness. We reviewed the program that I had made for my father's funeral services and noticed several mistakes, but my family overlooked them all and said, "Don't worry about it. We know you did the best you could with no rest."

The next day we buried my dad; it was a hard day for the entire family and many others in the community. I think many of my emotions came out that day; I cried to the Lord, fervently asking why, with great pain and tears. My brothers and sisters comforted me, saying, "We still have each other." I gathered my composure as we, the sons of Patsy Lee and Lee Earnest, took our pallbearer positions and carried my father's coffin to its proper place. So we got past that dark day and laid my dad to rest.

Chapter 31 Welcome to Tucson, Arizona

*M*any of the family members left soon afterward. Those of us who were heading west checked all of our things that night and were getting ready to sleep for a few hours before taking off when the phone rang. It was one of our uncles calling to tell us that our Uncle Robert had died from a heart attack on the way back home. We were not able to go to his funeral, and we headed to our destinations. I stayed in Tucson with my brother, John L., and attended the University of Arizona. I enrolled in the general studies program with concentrations in math, computer science, and black history. I bought a cheap car and picked up a job. I met with the dean of the general studies department and worked out a plan to graduate within one and a half years. The dean told me that I was taking on quite a bit and that I should not push so hard, but I told him that I had to because I had wasted too much time already.

I began to have dreams regularly, many of them about my father, my mission, and sometimes both. One dream was about me standing on a cloud and reaching down to pull others out of water beneath the clouds. In another dream my brother Eugene and I were guarding my father's body inside a glass building and Satan was coming in through a crack in the glass. We both had spears. Eugene charged Satan with his spear, and then it was just me, the body of my father, and Satán. I then pushed the spear into my Bible and ran into Satan. The room began to shake, and then I noticed that the glass walls were gone and so was the body of my father. Then I was all alone and I woke up. I had many such dreams.

In the meantime, my mind had been cleared and I was on the dean's list again. At this time, my sister, Eula, had an aneurism in Long Beach and the doctors gave no positive news, but we prayed as a family and asked churches across the country where we had family to do intercessory prayer. The report is that Eula is doing well today by the power of Jesus. At the end of the accelerated summer sessions of 1983, I stood in the dean's office being congratulated by him for finishing as we agreed. This was a happy time, but more than that, it was a time of victory for an underdog, a time of deliverance by the Lord. Even though I was still not right with him, he was carrying me, guiding and leading me to something and somewhere.

Because of issues with my brother's wife, I thought it prudent to move out. I thanked him for his love and belief in me and moved into a small house with one of my friends that I had met in my French studies. I began looking for a job utilizing my degree but could not find one. Even though my brother was an executive manager at IBM, nothing would shake loose there; I just didn't fit the model. Hughes Missile systems did not show any interest; nor could I find anything at Davis-Monthan Air Force Base. The only jobs that I could find were small part-time minimum-wage jobs and a handyman job that paid a little more. I was struggling to have meat on the table. Some of my jobs were on campus. I remember going to the bathroom and rolling off toilet paper to be used later at the small cottage because I couldn't afford to buy any or, when I went to a fast-food restaurant or cafeteria, taking the little bags of tea, sugar, and salt and pepper that were on the table. I lived on sardines and crackers; going to a fast food place like Church's Fried Chicken was a treat. When Christmas Eve came, my roommate and his brother gave me a gift for Christmas, but I had nothing to give to them. I cannot express the sadness I felt, and I burst out in tears and wondered what else I could do. That Christmas Eve, I thought about my life and accomplishments. I went to my room feeling down and defeated, and then I had a thought to call my sister Sanguretta.

Sanguretta listened to me complain about my troubles and problems and told me that I should come live with her and Sam (her husband) until I could find a job in my major. We began to plan this move, but since I didn't have much, it was an easy move. I sold my old car and a few more items, bought an airline ticket to Long Beach, and moved to stay with them the following week.

Chapter 32 A New Day in California

When I arrived in Long Beach, I was greeted by the rest of the family, to include my sister Geneva and her children, my oldest sister Eula and her son. There was a host of cousins—Cousin Lula Bell, Thelma, and Ollie—and their children, Carolyn and Tracy and others. It was such a great feeling to be surrounded by the love of family and not be alone. I felt very good but knew that I was there for a reason; therefore, I began to do a massive job search.

During those days, the Sunday paper was full of jobs. Computers were rare then, so I used an electronic typewriter to do my resumes and cover letter. I tried to help out around the house as best I could by cleaning up and cooking too. On the average, I sent out ten resumes a day. I was stone-broke and depended on Sam and Sanguretta to fund my job search. After one month, I had gotten a few responses but nothing significant, and I was feeling down, but my oldest sister, Eula, told me that I had no reason to be down. She told me that God was working and needed me to keep working as well. So I took my big sister's advice and worked harder to send out more resumes. About a week later, I received a call from a manager named Tom from ITT/FEC at Vandenberg AFB. Tom gave me a phone interview and said that someone from the HR department would be calling me before the week ended. That same week, I also had a phone interview with Redland Hill Academy (a computer technology school).

On Thursday of that week, I received another call from the ITT/FEC HR department. They called me Mr. Coker, which was really startling. Nobody called me mister. That title was for old people and the white people of the South. The lady from the HR department told me that on behalf of ITT/FEC, she was prepared to make me an offer. She then said, "How does 19,000 dollars per year sound?" The year was 1984, and to me, this was quite bit of money considering what I had made and was currently making. I was so surprised and amazed that my response was "Are you joking?" The lady from HR took it to mean that I was saying that it wasn't enough and went to ask her management about a counteroffer. She then said, "We can go to 21,000 dollars as our final offer. This time, I held my excitement, gathered my composure, and said, "I accept your offer."

She then asked when could I start, and my reply was "Monday." She told me that was really soon but that I could do a physical when I came to Lompoc. HR told me that they would book me a hotel room in Lompoc for the following Sunday. I got off the phone and shouted to the Lord with joy. I then called Sanguretta and told her of the good news. She called Sam, and they began to make plans to get me to Vandenberg AFB that Sunday. So we told the rest of the family and my oldest sister, Eula, through a family party that Saturday to celebrate how God had provided once again.

Sunday finally came, and I was surprised by Sam when he said, "We are going to give you the old car that we own." Off to Lompoc we went that morning. When we got to the hotel, they had no reservation for me, and I began to panic, but Sam said these kinds of things happened all the time. He used his credit card to guarantee me a room and gave me a credit card and told me, "Here, use this card if you have to." This meant and still means much to me. That was Sam; he has always been and still is a giving man who is always willing to help family members who were interested in advancing. Even now, sometimes, tears surface when I think of his kindness and generosity.

Monday I went to Vandenberg AFB and found ITT/FEC. I met Tom, my new manager, and went through a brief orientation. I didn't want to use my brother-in-law's credit card and had little money, so my plan was to eat peanut butter and jelly sandwiches and fruit and sardines for dinner until I got my first check. On my third day of the job, a coworker asked me why I was eating peanut butter and jelly sandwiches every day. I replied that I didn't have any money besides gas money. He then told me that I should fill out a form with ITT/FEC to borrow a few hundred dollars, which could be paid back in increments from my future paychecks. He also told me that employee of ITT/FEC could run an open tab with the hotel that I was living in. I got a five-hundred-dollar loan so that I could put the deposit down on an apartment and have a little spending money. That night I went to the hotel and had steak and lobster for dinner. So for all to know: **YAHWEH Jireh** – *"The Lord provides."*

I loved working for ITT/FEC at Vandenberg AFB, and because I had never had a real job before, I was extremely motivated to do well in my new position. It was exciting writing software to test missile launches and see the result of your work with each missile launch (as long as they went in the right direction). I even had medical and dental insurance included with my benefits and was automatically enrolled in a retirement plan. I immediately took advantage of these benefits by working with a local dentist to get my teeth fixed. My teeth had been a nagging problem of mine every since I could remember. Many children had belittled and teased my about my teeth throughout the years.

Reviewing the X-rays, the dentist thought I had a tumor in the roof of my mouth because there was a mass above the tooth line. So with great fear, I sought the Lord while the dentist took more X-rays and culture samples. When I went back, he was extremely happy and told me, "We know what it is!" He then asked me if I had been in an accident or somehow damaged my teeth. I told him that I had run into an iron swing set when I was four or five. The dentist told me that the permanent teeth were still there and high above my gum line and that was the mass that he saw but could not make it out because of their positioning. He then told me that I could have them pulled down a little bit every two weeks for the next year or have them surgically removed and put a bridge in. I was much more impatient then than now and chose option B. Now that I am older, I wish I had chosen option A, but that's the way it is sometimes. At least it wasn't a tumor. God had delivered me once again, and in the end, no one would be able to call me Snaggletooth again.

I joined Grace Temple Baptist church in Lompoc and became active in the men's ministry and one year coordinated the church's activity at the Lompoc flower festival. Lompoc was a small town, and many people went to Santa Maria to do serious shopping since Santa Maria had a mall. I enjoyed living in Lompoc, but there wasn't much there for singles. There were a lot of married military wives who were starving for attention in the absence of their husbands. Contractors were allowed to go to the officers' club and NCOIC club for discos. Besides that there was only one disco in Lompoc. Many of the married women would take their rings off and lie about their marital status. Then there were the older women in church who were interested in temporary relationships. Soon you got to know everybody and the game got tiring. While in Lompoc, I decided to get another degree—this time a degree in computer engineering from Chapman College. There was an extension of Chapman College at Vandenberg AFB that offered a degree program.

A few years later, I got a job in Huntington Beach and moved to Norwalk, California, which was only a few miles from Sanguretta and Sam and within a ten-mile radius of my other sisters, Eula and Geneva. The last few years had been spent living the bachelor life and always on the go, but it was great to be around so much family without the poverty. My work was in military intelligence, and I never spoke of what I did; people who knew me just said that I was one of those computer people. I was still in the single lifestyle, and even though I had plenty of family in the Long Beach area, I was quite lonely at times. I went through failed relationship after failed relationship.

Two of my best friends, JD and Jeanne, were getting married in Selma, Alabama. I met up with Sam, Angie, JD and Jeanne, and others in Selma for this great event. During this time, I met a young lady, Mildred, who was very kind and grounded. After the wedding, we spent hours talking to each other, but there were no sparks. Mildred then told me that her best friend was going to be moving to Long Beach shortly, but I took it lightly, and she said it again as if to imply that this friend of hers was the one for me. I didn't have to guess if that's what she meant because she came right out and said, "I have no doubt that you all are a perfect match." Mildred made me promise to be nice when she called and give the relationship a chance.

A few months later, Cynthia, the friend of Mildred, called and we met. It was good to be talking to someone from back home that had lived where I lived and really understood the culture, food, and Christian upbringing. We hit it off right away and became very close. We made one major mistake by becoming sexually involved rather than waiting until after getting married. Cynthia became pregnant, and we had big decisions to make. I was going to be moving to New Jersey on a one-to-two-year job assignment with the army. Neither of us wanted to be separated; nor did we want to become another negative statistic in the black community. Therefore, we decided to get married.

We broke the news of this to our families and asked for their support. There were a few questions posed to us, but the general consensus was very supportive. We received counseling from the pastor of St. John's Lutheran Church and Cynthia's father as well, who had been a Lutheran pastor for more than thirty years. My sisters, led by chief chef Eula, put a plan in place for the food and cake, etc. On December 27, 1986, we were married by my father-in-law, Pastor Moses Julius Clark.

Shortly afterward, we moved to New Jersey in Eatontown, where I supported the Military Intelligence (MI) division of Fort Mammoth. Certain contractual agreements made by the company that I worked for were not honored and my manager, who was still in Huntington Beach, took no interest in helping me solve these issues. We ended up losing thousands of dollars on this from money that we did not have.

On July 7, 1987, Nathan, our first child, was born, but because Cynthia developed high blood pressure and toxemia, an emergency C-section had to be performed. As I sat in the waiting room, I thought of the danger that I had put Cynthia and Nathan in by bringing them to this new place and not being able to be around. I thought about how we were arguing all the time and how she was spending so much time alone in the small, cramped hotel room. This was not a time that I am proud of, and if I could have one wish that I could go back in time, it would be to treat her as Christ would want me to and prioritize my choices correctly.

Finally, the doctor came out and said, "You are the father of a baby boy." I asked about Cynthia and the doctor said that she would be sedated for a few hours and would need to stay in the hospital a few more weeks. I went in to see Cynthia, but she was not conscious. A few minutes after that, a group of soldiers tasked by the MI commander came to the hospital to get me. I told them that my wife had just delivered and had to stay in the hospital a few weeks and that I could not come. They then told me, "You don't understand. You must come with us or there will be trouble for you and us." So I rationalized following them. When we got to the site, I did what I could, but due to a storm, there was some damaged equipment that had to be replaced. I then had to report to the MI commander. I reported to him the status and went back to the hospital, but when I went to Cynthia's room, she was already awake and very angry with me and could not understand why I wasn't there.

The next few years were the roughest years of our married life. One time Cynthia left me and went home; at the same time the military was continuing to be very demanding. Eventually I was able to get the contractual issues resolved with the company that I worked for and decided to move back to Southern California. Cynthia and Nathan moved back, but I had to stay in New Jersey until a replacement could be found. After about four months, I returned to my family, and Ashley, my daughter, was born on April 10, 1989. We were having serious financial problems, which complicated our other internal relationship problems. We decided to look to see what we could afford in the purchase of our first home. We qualified for 96,000 dollars and found ourselves in the middle of gang and prostitute territory. There was no budget-squeezing possible to get us into the type of home or neighborhood that we wanted to have. The viewpoint was not to look down or criticize those who lived in such neighborhoods. If it were up to me, no one would live in a place where they didn't feel safe or had to worry about the safety and direction of their children.

There was a management position available with my company for someone who had MI Imagery experience. This was one of my specialties. I had the required government configuration management control skills. I had not one bachelor's degree but two and was working on an MBA. My manager didn't want me to have this position; he had it marked for another white guy who went to lunch with him but who did not satisfy the job requirements. I questioned him on the subject, and he told me that I wasn't going to get the position regardless of my qualifications. I stormed out of his office and went to the office of the deputy director of the division and waited to see him. I went in and spilled my guts. He had my file pulled, reviewed it, and said, "You are definitely qualified. If you don't sue us, I can find you another management position." I told him that I really appreciated hearing him say that, but if I was qualified for the imagery management position, I should get it. He agreed and told me to take the rest of the day off and give him a few weeks.

I went home, and when Cynthia saw me, she asked if I had been fired. I asked her why she thought I would be fired, and she yelled at me to just tell her what had happened. As I was telling her, a friend from work called and told me about a major job fair at the Long Beach Marriot. He was a Christian and told me that I could sue if I wanted to, but he said that he thought that Cynthia and I should pray about at the job fair and that I should direct the energy behind my anger toward getting a job. I got off the phone and we prayed, as was suggested. I put on my suit and headed for the Marriot. When I got there, there were people everywhere, but I stayed focused, asked the Lord to help me do well, and started interviewing. Within a span of four hours, I had a soft job offer from three companies. There were no cell phones at that time, and though I wanted to call Cynthia, I also wanted to tell her in person.

When I got home, she knew it was good by the smile on my face. I told her that we had a choice of San Diego, Las Vegas, or Sierra Vista. We didn't know which to take, but depending on the offers, were favoring Sierra Vista, Arizona because my brother John lived in Tucson and had been very ill. The offer from Martin Marietta was a 42 percent increase from what I was currently making, but was only guaranteed for one year. So we took it and moved to Sierra Vista, Arizona. Truly God had smiled on us once again and we began to try to resolve a tough issue, finding a church. Even after being in Sierra Vista, I didn't fully understand the full scope of God's blessing on us. It was Labor Day, and Cynthia said, "Let's go look at houses." My reply was that we couldn't afford to buy anything, but she was always more optimistic than me and said, "Then you have nothing to worry about. Let's go." I took her to the golf course first, thinking that going there would stop this fantasy she was having, but to my surprise, one of the most beautiful homes at the golf course was only $160,000. I then asked the realtor what kind of house could we get for around 90,000 dollars? We were told that we could get a very nice home with many options. I saw then that my wife had a certain degree of hope that I was lacking but needed because without hope we cannot obtain the things of God or enjoy the abundance of his blessings that he freely gives, whether we are operating in his will or not. On that Labor Day, through the help of my wife, I was able to see and embrace fully the blessing that God gave us in Sierra Vista with this new job.

Six months later, we purchased our first home and learned that we were expecting our third child, and on September 3, 1990, Derrick was born. By now, we were visiting two churches in Sierra Vista, the local Missouri Senate Lutheran church and St. Paul Missionary Baptist church. I attended many of the Bible classes in the Lutheran church, and many took me to be a good Lutheran. Cynthia's parents were putting a lot of pressure on her to stay Lutheran. One Sunday we had a really bad argument. After that, I went to church at St. Paul, and after the pastor's sermon, someone sat beside me. I looked and it was Cynthia. She told me that it was time for us to join a church together and that she was ready to join St. Paul. All I could do was cry because I didn't understand what was going on. We joined St. Paul that day, and Cynthia was baptized at Antioch Baptist, which is located in Huachuca City. We worked hard in this church and became very close to the other members. Many there said they could sense an anointing of God on me, but I was still hesitant to make any sudden changes.

My job was still in MI at Fort Huachuca, and I traveled quite a bit, and once again Cynthia was alone with the kids too much. I struggled to give her the time that she deserved, which caused problems in our relationship. I remember telling her that she needed to do more to organize her career, which caused more problems. Later she told me that she wanted to work with computers as I did. I didn't see where she was coming from (she only said that to show me that she wanted to have time with me, thinking that working in that field would bring us closer together), so I made the situation worse by saying something stupid. After me sleeping on the couch a few nights, she came to me and said, "I want to be a nurse". Looking into Cynthia's eyes, I could tell that this was something that she wanted to do. At that time, we began planning to make it happen.

Cynthia took prerequisite classes at Cochise Jr. College and applied to the nursing school at the University of Arizona. Most people we knew said that she would have to apply a few times before getting accepted, but we were a prodigy of God providing for His people and went down on our knees in prayer, asking Him for another victory by opening a door that many said was closed. Within a few weeks of Cynthia applying, she received a letter from the university saying "Congratulations on your acceptance to the University of Arizona School of Nursing." We immediately told our pastor about this and gave a testimony in church. Some then said that she was only accepted the first try because she was black, but the majority of people didn't see it that way and rejoiced with us. We then began to plan how she would attend school in Tucson while the rest of the family was in Sierra Vista (which is about seventy-five miles from Tucson). Cynthia suggested that she should move to Tucson and come home during the weekends. I didn't like that idea at all; we were talking two-plus years. Therefore, we decided to move the family to Tucson and I would drive back to Fort Huachuca to my job daily.

Within the first year of this, I was also working in the ministry in a local Tucson church but knew that I had to do something else. So I began to seek the Lord for my purpose and persistently asked him to use me, to take me and direct me to be of service for the cause of the Gospel of Jesus Christ. Early one morning, on the third day of my praying and fasting for this purpose, I was on my way to Fort Huachuca. It was still dark, and I was listening at a song play on my tape, "Yes, God is Real." At some point during this song, the tears began to roll down my face and I felt myself in the presence of a magnificent presence. That presence was the spirit of the Lord and as I looked at the elements of the environment, I received spiritual knowledge and understanding from God. For every bush, tree, mountain, etc., and the rising of the sun that I saw, related passages were being fed to my spirit. Before I knew it, I was at work in Fort Huachuca. The message I took from this was that it was time for me to preach the gospel. I tried to work that day, but I just could not and returned home. From that point on, I increased my efforts by teaching others and educating myself within the ministry.

After a year of driving to Fort Huachuca five days a week, I saw myself burning out. Cynthia was still attending the university, and I was teaching or going to class four days a week while picking up the kids and taking care of their needs. I tried carpooling and taking the bus, but due to my busy schedule, I had to drive. I thank God that the kids never got sick and were dependent on me coming from Sierra Vista to pick them up. I was in the middle of teaching a class at church about effective prayer and told Cynthia that we needed to pray to God for a job for me in Tucson.

We got on our knees and prayed this prayer:

> *Oh God, great Jehovah, throughout the years you have truly been our all and all. You have been our shelter, our rock, and mighty fortress. We need a job for me in Tucson so that I can continue working in the ministry and be here for my family. Thank you, Lord, because we know you hear our prayers in the name of Jesus. Amen.*

I planned my interview strategy and prepared a presentation for all of my interviews. IBM turned their nose up at me, and Hughes Missile plant was not hiring. I received an offer from the Pima County district attorney's office, which was only half of what they had advertised. They said that they had made a mistake in the ad. I sought the advice of my new pastor from the Tucson church, and he told me that I should take it and not be greedy. That night I told Cynthia about it and she became very stressed, as I already was. We had gone into debt by more than 20,000 dollars for her to go to the university, and we depended on childcare. There was no way I could take a 50 percent pay cut, and then I looked at the cover of one of the books that I was using in my Bible class, *The Fourth Dimension*, by Dr. Paul Choi, and it hit me like a ton of bricks. We didn't tell God the desires of our heart. More specifically, we were not specific with God. With great excitement, I took Cynthia's hand and said, "Let's pray again." This time, we prayed:

Oh God, great Jehovah, throughout the years you have truly been our all and all. You have been our shelter, our rock and mighty fortress. We did not ask you, as we should have for the blessing of a job here in Tucson. Lord, I need a job here in Tucson, working for the same company that I work for now, that pays the same amount, and if possible, Lord, allow me to work at the Hughes or IBM facility. Oh, Lord, we give you the praise and glory. Amen.

That next Sunday in church, one of the deacons who worked at Hughes told me that my company, CSC (replacing Martin Marietta in Sierra Vista), had gotten some work in the Hughes engineering department. That Monday I inquired with HR and got the name of the proper CSC manager and called him. I told him who I was and that I was applying for job openings that he had. He told me that he had no job openings. My reply was, "I believe you will. Please review and keep my resume handy." He told me that it was CSC's policy to keep all resumes on file for six months. Cynthia and I kept praying and having hope.

217

The next day, about noon, I was called by this manager, who said, "I don't know how you knew, but we got one opening here in Tucson in the Tomahawk Lab. This is amazing. While the current lab manager was quitting, I looked down and saw your resume and remembered my conversation with you. The job is yours if you are still interested. Your pay will be the same and you will be working out of the Hughes facility and maybe the IBM building." I kept my cool and hung up the phone and shouted, "God is good." Others came to my desk to see what was happening. I told them, and there was just great amazement, shock, and awe. At the end of the day, a few people from the building came to me and asked me to pray for them. This made me feel strange, but I did it anyway and told them that their prayers were and are what was needed for their situations. Within a few weeks, I was working in Tucson at the Hughes and IBM buildings. Cynthia and I thanked God greatly and gave our testimony at the church. As the years went by, I had the opportunity to preach regularly in churches other than my home church in Tucson. The job continued at Hughes (which became Raytheon) from year to year.

Chapter 33 Adversity Never Stops

*D*uring these years, the health of my brother John was declining. One week, while in Fort Lauderdale, Florida, at a training class, I received a call from my sister-in-law informing me that John was connected to life support and the doctors had given up on him. I called my boss, informed him of my situation, and caught the next flight home. I went straight to the hospital to see him. There were members from different churches there praying in the halls and in his room. He saw me there and gave me a thumbs-up. I spoke with the doctor and was told that they could do no more dialysis on him and that the multiple problems that he had were just to much to overcome. Early in the morning, I arrived home and gave Cynthia the latest status.

A few days later, John died. His wife asked me to help take care of the arrangements. Once again, I was put in a similar situation as that with my father. I couldn't help but think of the time when my father had died and was put to rest. John had already asked Sanguretta and me some time earlier, to help my sister-in-law with her finances. We were determined to do this and satisfy a promise made to our departed brother. So we wasted no time in getting this started and attempting to make help by aligning up all the insurance policies and assets.

At the same time, Cynthia's finals exams were scheduled for that week, and one instructor declined to allow Cynthia to postpone her final exam. It was necessary to go to the dean to get this exam postponed—not an extremely difficult thing to do, but it should not have been necessary under the circumstances. Others had gotten postponements for things with less justification. After overcoming this hurdle, there were other obstacles, one right after another.

As my family was getting into town for the funeral, they had planned to stay at John's home; many of them wanted to do this for sentimental reasons and to provide assistance to my sister-in-law. One night they called me and asked me to come and get them. I led them all back over to my house, except for James (my oldest brother) and his family. They had been told that they should go stay with me in order to make room for my sister-in-law's family. It didn't get any better trying to make arrangements at the funeral home. The mortician tried to talk down to us, so you can imagine how that went, but my sister-in-law took his side against us.

At one point, the wife of the mortician said, "This happens a lot when we work with black folks." I replied, "What are you talking about? You are just as black as the rest of us, and the only reason that we are here is to help two black people, you and your husband." This was just a bad time because it even caused some of the sisters and brothers to be at each other's throats. You learn that when a love one dies, those remaining struggle to cope with the situation left behind. I just wanted it to be over. When the day of the funeral came, it was like two separate families. All of my sister-in-law's family crawled into the family cars. Many of John's siblings drove, while a few others managed to get into one of the family cars. Seating at the church was chaotic, as well as at the burial site. (I had to ask some of the men to give up family seating at the burial site so that the sisters could at least sit down under the burial tent.) I thought to myself, most of these people didn't really know him or spend any time with him and now they qualify as prime-time family?

It was truly a dark day in our family history, but it didn't stop there; just wanted it to all be over. I was committed to completing a promise that I had made to my brother by helping his wife get her finances in order. One day, in the parking lot of a First Interstate Bank, she told me that she did not know if she could trust me anymore. I could not think of a worse time. My brother had died, and I had not had a chance to properly grieve because of helping her and taking care of the business at hand. I was not able to respond to her. All I could do was go home to Cynthia like a beaten dog with my tail between my legs. I had been beaten and labeled as untrustworthy by someone whom I loved very much—just like a sister. I called Sanguretta and told her about it, and I remember her telling me that I had no choice but to let it go and consider my promise to John complete. It took some time for things to get better. I thank my nephew, Dale, for keeping the communication going. We have come a long way and much I attribute to him and his wife Edna. I am clearly thankful to have them near.

It was about six months before I could really grieve. Within this time, Cynthia graduated with honorable mention from the school of nursing and started working immediately. Within the next year, I was ordained as a Baptist pastor and began seeking God for more details.

One day I had packed my luggage for a business trip to San Francisco and headed out the door to drop the kids off to school. I prayed with them, hugged them, and told them, "Don't take any wooden nickels." Up to this time, I had never worn seat beats consistently, but my daughter, on this day, reached across me, grabbed my seat beat, fastened it, and said, "Dad, promise you will wear your seat belt!" I said yes to her, and I was off to the office for a few hours before boarding my flight. As I was approaching the Tucson Pima Air Museum, a tan Pathfinder zoomed into my lane from the left lane. I glanced at the driver and passenger and could tell that they were not paying any attention to what they were doing. I tried to blow my horn but rushed to avoid the collision, as I was in a small four-door Daihatsu. I avoided the collision with the Pathfinder but hit the curve and flipped over.

There I was on Valencia Road, sliding in the street upside down during the morning rush hour. There was gas leaking from a ruptured gas tank and glass and fire sparks flying around my face, some popping against my eyeglasses. All of this was happening in seconds, but it seemed like eternity. I started talking to the Lord. I said:

Oh, God, I thank you for all blessings, small and large. Thank you for blessing me with Cynthia and my children. Please, God,

have mercy on me, but if I don't make it this time, please, Master, take care of my family.

A few minute later, the car stop spinning and sliding down the road, but was still upside down. I heard the gospel music playing on the tape of my car and the sound of footsteps running toward the car. There was the sound of women crying and men telling their children not to look. One of the men approached the car, stooped down, and asked, "Can you speak?" I said, "Yes, I am all right" and unsnapped my seatbelt and dropped down to the top of the car, which was now the bottom. I leaned out of the car and laid on my back facing the sunlight and said, "God is good." Someone handed me my work bag, which was smoking because of being dragged about thirty yards. The car was totaled, with three out of four corners caved in; the only one left was where I was sitting in the car.

I was strapped to a stretcher and put in the ambulance. All my vitals were normal; the paramedics were making jokes that I must have been dead before the accident since my blood pressure was 120/70. I was taken to a local hospital and spent the morning there. I went ahead and boarded that flight to San Francisco, carrying my workbag, which had been dragged down the road in the accident. Many asked me questions about the bag or about a fragment of glass that might have been on my person; I used each as a way of testifying about the grace and mercy of God. God used my baby girl to save me and provided the answer to my prayer before I ever prayed the prayer. If I had not had my seat beat on, I would have had the same fate as my workbag.

It is significant here to mention that obedience and keeping your commitment is necessary in order to benefit from your prayers. God put it on my daughter's heart to make sure her dad had his seat beat fastened on that day. Furthermore, she made her dad promise to keep it fastened. I cannot let an opportunity pass without mentioning Ephesians, chapter six: "Put on the whole armor of God." That day God gave me a personal example, which I lived through so that others could be blessed. Many said that God was trying to tell me I needed to straighten up, and I resented it at the time, but I have learned that regardless of what they meant by it, I should always try to do better in serving the Lord.

We were also having trouble fitting in at our home church and saw that it was time to move on. I was halfway through completing a master's degree in ministry when I was called to interview for the pastor ship at a local Baptist church. Part of my curriculum at the Bible college was to develop a plan of ministry. This plan had to be developed and researched in accordance with the scripture and the laws of the state. It was completed and was everything that I would need to develop a church.

The congregation loved me, my family, and especially the plan and steps to move the ministry, but the lead deacon, the leaving pastor, and another pastor did not like it because it challenged many traditional ideas, which had nothing to do with salvation. One major difference was that I had no problem with women being in the ministry in leadership roles, but they did. I had written papers on the topic from a biblical perspective and presented them with my works, but it didn't matter. I was told by them that there was no way that they would ever believe anything different than what they already believed and that there was no way that I would get to pastor that church. I told them that it seemed like they were "leaning to their own understanding."

The following Monday, the church congregation was scheduled to vote on it, but according to several members who called me afterward, the leaders had prevented the vote from occurring. From that point on, I never went to that church again; I withdrew my name, and my family joined a nondenominational Christian church. We joined this church because the senior pastor had committed to assisting us in planting a church on the southeast side of Tucson. Cynthia and I committed to this ministry, but more than a year went by and the senior pastor had not come through on any of his promises.

I continued praying and fasting from time to time, and with twenty people, we opened the House of the Lord in Tucson. We started having services in our home and after a few months moved the services to the Hilton. On the first day of service, another church opened with their first service at the Hilton as well, but they had much more support from a sponsoring church. There was a busload of people who had come from California to help them. They moved out of the hotel before us to different locations but had good support. I learned from this that having the assistance of another church is essential for success.

Then there were some who came to the House of the Lord in Tucson, running from their previous church. If you are a struggling pastor out there, don't take them! They are poison to the body. One searching family insisted that we make the church a black church. I totally rejected this thought and stated that the church belongs to Jesus and we should accommodate all people. I just wanted workers who cared about other people and who wanted to share the grace of their faith with others. Then there were the leaders who always seemed to talk a big talk but never showed up. The second significant point here is that the core of any ministry must have a majority of strong Christians who care about the vision as much as the pastor and are willing to sacrifice as needed for its success. There were a few who were really committed; I wish they could have been cloned.

I made the mistake of going with the idea of moving the church to the southwest side of town, believing that my work was to be on the southeast side. I should have stuck to my belief regardless. Everything that I had been taught indicated that the church should be in the neighborhood of the key leaders and at least the pastor or they should move to the neighborhood.

But you know what? I was so used to God saying yes to me and Cynthia that I was sure He was going to say yes to the House of the Lord in Tucson. All of those things that I mentioned previously about the church are secondary. I even blamed God in my mind at times, which I have repented, but the fact was that I preached the faith of "Shadrach, Meshach, and Abed-Nego" but had to live and learn the most critical point. These young men said that they would remain committed to the Almighty whether He delivered them or not. In other words, delivering them had nothing to do with them walking through the fire untouched by its flame. The key point from the closing of the House of the Lord in Tucson for Pastor Coker is to never think you know God better than He knows you. Know that He can always say no and that your commitment to Him must always be yes.

Chapter 34 *Moving On*

---

*F*or the last few years, Cynthia and I have been working on a plan to get out of debt. There is a Bible verse, Romans 13:8: *"Owe no one anything except to love one another, for he who loves another has fulfilled the law."* This is not to imply that God has a rule and you are damned if in debt. (We would be there with everyone else.) For us, getting out of debt frees us up from the banker, "and the borrower is servant to the lender," (Proverbs 22:7).

Early on in our marriage, we had to ask ourselves who we were working for: God, the banker, or ourselves. Yes, we are committed to tithing and have been since living in Sierra Vista. Prior to this commitment, we gave regularly, but not a specific amount or in a systematic way. Through the years, we looked at where our financial resources were going, and determined that the banker was getting more than his fair share. We took the class Financial Peace University created by Dave Ramsey. This was a great blessing and was Bible-based. I recommend everyone take such a class so that you can be empowered over the finances that you manage for God. Since taking this class, we are well on our way to giving much beyond the 10 percent in tithing and establishing a sound financial foundation.

Outside the norm, there are times when we donate to other charities that we have not budgeted for, but it comes out of the same budget. We still use credit on a very limited basis and like it to be to our advantage rather than the bankers. If you are interested in such things, take my advice and take the class.

The significance of working to be debt-free is that it will bring you so many options. Cynthia is currently working as a nurse section leader, and I am a senior computer scientist and ordained pastor. Our goal within the next three to five years is to be in a position to do mission work. It is good to have a plan, and we have one, but I have learned that God's plan can take you in a totally different direction. In either case, having little or no debt liabilities is the place that you want to be. The other part of Romans 13:8, "*for he who loves another has fulfilled the law,*" is not compromising.

When I was a child, I was taught that we had to obey the law of the Bible, but I learned a few years later that those who love God must love mankind or they don't love God. We are working hard to push forward this idea. As we grow in Christ, we are led to believe that this must be the direction of the ministry in which we work, along with the truth of God as an absolute.

Looking back to where I first started, I am indeed grateful to God for every experience, whether labeled good or bad, because all of my experiences have contributed to where I am today. My dad taught me a very important principle when I was little. He said, "Keep God first, love your family, and be the best at what you do." I thank him, and have not always practiced this as I should, but I know that for me this is the mark of success. This is the mark that I strive for each day—the mark that he gave me early on. Money is good to have, and God has blessed me such that we have never been begging for bread, but it can all disappear in a second. So having it is not a good measurement of success. To be respected in the community is a good thing; we may have that respect, depending on who you talk to, but to be recognized by the Lord for love of others is better. I have learned that success on the job is worth mentioning, but it's temporary and has no everlasting effect. This I have experienced as well. Success can't primarily be placed in or on your family either; only when God is put first can you see the family as part of your success.

I have learned to be faithful to my family also. Personal family time is critical; we always made (and continue to do so) a big deal of going on vacations. Years back, we started saving for vacation just like we did for our retirement. Sometimes we didn't have much, but we managed to take the kids on a shorter trip or to a closer place, like Phoenix or Sierra Vista, or on a drive to Bisbee. Many of the places had no TV, radio, or phones; these places were the best because they forced us to play games together, go fishing or hiking, etc. One time, I was working on some things from my job on a vacation trip when one of my kids said, "Dad, don't you have time for us? You said that vacations are for fun and no work." I got the message, put all the papers away, and began to give them horseback rides. I have seen many pastors neglect their families for the sake of the ministry, but believe that God wants the whole family working as one unit for the kingdom. The relationships that we make with others, including those in the church, are based on the type of relationships we have within our own family. If others see you and your family as a tight unit, it speaks to your credibility and testimony.

Success is not based on size or the number in your church but the heartbeat of the congregation, the health of the church. So once again, the advice from my dad has had everlasting merit to it. Putting God first makes all the difference in this world and in next one too.

So now, I look back over my life and say, thank you Father because you have made a way for me and my family even when it seemed hopeless at time; my God made a way. I have come a long way from Sardis, Alabama, and yet I look forward to the journey that God has prepared ahead. I am still seeking the Lord to be a better servant of exercising myself for His purpose. With God as my strength, I will finish this race.

Printed in the United States
136767LV00001B/6/A

9 781434 325648